Includes step-by-step guide for
individual or group activities

Reimagine
YOUR RETIREMENT

How to LIVE Life
to its FULLEST and
Leave a Lasting LEGACY

Joyce Y. Li

REIMAGINE YOUR RETIREMENT

ISBN: 978-1-77069-771-3

Printed in Canada

Word Alive Press
~~131 Cordite Road~~, Winnipeg, MB R3W 1S1
www.wordalivepress.ca

WORD ALIVE PRESS
Just Write!

Library and Archives Canada Cataloguing in Publication

Li, Joyce Y., 1958-
Reimagine your retirement : how to live life to its fullest and leave a lasting legacy / Joyce Y. Li.

ISBN 978-1-77069-771-3

1. Retirement--Planning. I. Title.

HQ1062.L5 2013 646.7'9 C2012-907597-3

dedication

This book is dedicated to God,
our Heavenly Father, to whom all glory is due.

To Philip,
my better half; through him God's grace is displayed.

To Mom and Dad,
my devoted parents; through their sacrificial love I was raised.

To Ginny and Samuel, Amanda, Michelle, and Isaac,
my lovely angels on earth; through them God's blessings are bestowed.

table of contents

introduction vii

Part One

RECOGNIZE THE MANY POSSIBILITIES **1**

ONE: What Does Retirement Mean to You? 3

TWO: Redefine Your Retirement 19

Part Two

LIVING YOUR BEST **45**

THREE: Aging Gracefully in Body, Mind, and Spirit 47

FOUR: Why Planning Works For the Long Haul 71

Part Three

DISCOVERING YOURSELF **81**

FIVE: What Does the Bible Say About His Plan for Your Life? 83

SIX: Defining Your Life Gifts 93

SEVEN: Identifying Your Personality, Strengths, and Weaknesses 115

EIGHT: Revitalize Your Passion 135

Part Four

VISION AND CALLING **145**

NINE: Visualize To Achieve 147

TEN: What Is Your Calling? 165

Part Five

PUT LEGS TO YOUR PLAN **185**

ELEVEN: The Three Steps To Success 187

TWELVE: Make Your Commitment 203

endnotes 209

acknowledgements 215

about the author 217

introduction

On July 16, 1997, I came home from the hospital after saying goodbye to my father on his deathbed. My eight-year-old daughter Amanda saw my gloomy expression and blurted, "Mommy, what happened? You look sad!"

I sobbed as I announced that Grandpa just passed away. Curiosity struck her and she asked why.

"He's old," I explained.

She responded quickly, "Mommy, you are also old. When are you gonna die?"

Now, fifteen years later, Amanda is asking me another question: "Mom, when are you going to retire?"

Let me ask you this: what comes to your mind when you hear or see the word retirement? Rocking chair? Golfing? Fishing? How about these words and phrases: disengage, depart, recline, exit, withdrawn, ageism, boring, hit the hay, hit the sack… Unfortunately, many people perceive negative connotations to retirement, such as the physical and mental decline that comes with aging. These include the adages:

- The old brain can't learn new tricks.
- You're too old to change.

- Your genes dictate how fast you age.
- You could do nothing to alter the negative side effect of aging.

But guess what? These are myths! They clash with scientific findings. Researchers from the MacArthur Foundation Study[1] have learned that lifestyle choices in food and exercise, plus challenging mental activities and social belongings, contribute to longevity and aging gracefully. It's never too late to make these choices and begin to see a difference.

I am 54 years old. According to Canadian statistics, I am expected to live an active life for another 20 or 30 years. Those images and descriptions of retirement are not what I have in mind for my future years.

I asked myself, how will I live life to the fullest by the time I reach 83? I struggled answering the query and began pondering how I want to see myself in the next 30 years.

This led me to make a commitment to live life with intention and intensity. Since then, I have been scouring bookstores for resources that would take me from discovering who I am and finding out God's plan in my life, to defining my life mission and having the vitality to live it out. Though it was a fun exploration, rewarding and meaningful, I can't tell if I'm living out my life mission, or simply achieving good deeds or pre-defined goals. While I desire for many to live out their special calling in life, I realized the need for practical tools that offer a complete package to guide this process.

Facing a higher life expectancy and plenty of resources, baby boomers like me have the golden opportunity to achieve greater things in their second half of life. *Reimagine Your Retirement* is the culmination of my own journey in fulfilling my calling to inspire, equip, and mobilize people to live life to its fullest. This book draws on lessons learned from both my formal and informal education, along with 30 years of professional experience from my roles as a programmer, department manager, teacher, workshop facilitator, counselor, and project manager.

The maker of this universe designed each one of us as a masterpiece. I call Him God, the heavenly Father. He loves us immensely. He desires everyone to know Him, love Him, and live life to the fullest. He longs for us to abide in Him as He waits patiently for us to build the most intimate relationship with Him.

Life on this earth is a journey. For believers, when the earthly journey is over, we will step into eternity where we will reside in the new heavens and new earth. We will have no pain, no sorrow, and no tears. We will spend eternity with our Creator, enjoying a joyful and peaceful relationship in heaven forever. Life on earth is only a dint in the horizon of eternity. Yet what we do here matters because our Creator is a God of purpose. He does things for a reason and nothing escapes His sight. Everything we do prepares us for wonders to come in the infinite state.

For now, we have the promise of an abundant life. In John 10:10, Jesus says, *"The thief comes only to steal and kill and destroy; I have come that they may have life, and have it to the full."* No matter where you are in this earthly journey, you can live your dream and experience greater purpose and fulfillment. I pray for you to experience the renewal of mind, as this book provides the resources to claim this promise. You will feel a new level of energy, enjoy greater peace, and unleash your personal best. Start reinventing your future. Your preparation for doing so involves three simple choices:

- An open mind
- A decision
- A commitment

It takes more than money to live a purposeful and fulfilling retirement. Many people finish their journey on earth with unrealized dreams, unaccomplished goals, under-utilized potentials, and unresolved conflicts. Living life to its fullest and leaving a lasting legacy requires you to consciously review some facts, discover yourself, craft a vision for the future, and formulate a roadmap to get there.

This book will show you how to attain all those factors for your better half of life. You will embrace your life with hope, vitality, and an exciting action plan. With convenience in mind, this book is a step-by-step how-to resource. I created this material originally as an interactive workshop series for baby boomers two years ago, and expanded it into this book for any adults considering their retirement future. So I will work with you chapter by chapter; you're not just flipping the pages from front to back. You will read, pause, pray, and ponder on questions; then you'll have opportunities to write your responses to each question, check off worksheets, fill in the self-discovery tools, highlight content that resonates with you, and jot down personal comments. Working through this book will enable you to:

- Learn about your potential and become motivated to imagine your new reality;
- Discover who you are and celebrate your personality, passion, value, and life gifts—your natural ability to do something well based on your interests;
- Visualize success for the next five, 10 or 20 years; and
- Redefine your retirement, plan your next season of life, and put your plan into action.

Success is not measured by how much you know—it's what you do with what you know that counts. John Henry Cardinal Newman said, "To grow is to change, and to be perfect is to have changed often."[2] I challenge you to dream a bigger dream and grow to fulfill your dream.

With that said, let this journey begin…

If you can imagine it, you can achieve it. If you can dream it, you can become it.
–Dr. William Arthur Ward, American author

Now faith is confidence in what we hope for and assurance about what we do not see.
–Hebrews 11:1

Part One

RECOGNIZE THE MANY POSSIBILITIES

Pause, stretch, and smile. Learn about your potential and take charge of your future. Explore "retirement" from different perspectives and envision the many exciting possibilities that appeal to you.

one

WHAT DOES RETIREMENT MEAN TO YOU?

"Moses was a hundred and 20 years old when he died,
yet his eyes were not weak nor his strength gone."
–Deuteronomy 34:7

"We are what we imagine ourselves to be."
–Kurt Vonnegut Jr., American author

"The spiritual eyesight improves as the physical eyesight declines."
–Plato (429–347 BCE), philosopher

WITH SIX BIG SUITCASES OF CLOTHES AND THREE MEGA BAGS OF TOYS and souvenirs for relatives, my husband Philip and I, with our four-year-old daughter Ginny, landed at the Toronto Pearson International Airport. My brother-in-law Roden welcomed us as new immigrants after our 18-hour flight from Hong Kong to Ontario, Canada. Though we hadn't been in Canada for long, he took us to a Chinese restaurant because we missed our homeland's food already! That day was September 12, 1987. Canada has been home ever since. Wow, thinking back, 25 years flew by like a whirlwind!

Then in my late 20s, I focused on finding a job, establishing my new home, and raising my family with my husband. As a new immigrant with no Canadian work experience, finding a job had been a difficult task. Nonetheless, I was fortunate to land a position relevant to my information-technology skills and background. I vividly remember the conversations around the water-cooler on Mondays or Fridays; my coworkers bragged about their weekend trips to the cottages and how they went biking, camping, and partying. From my observations, excitement from these weekend excursions motivated them to endure another week at the office.

Being new to the Canadian culture, my attitude was quite different. I didn't take any vacations during my first five years in Canada. My work colleague once said, "Joyce, don't you have a life outside the office? Take your children to the Algonquin Provincial Park—it's beautiful there! You can go biking, swimming, fishing, or just rest your feet and relax." Thinking back, these were actually words of wisdom. There is much to explore outside my job.

A Time to Build and Grow

Working is the means to an end. When I moved to Canada, my end goal was to build a stable family and afford a comfortable living. My coworkers included leisure and family fun as part of their lifestyles, explaining how penciling in downtime was important. You know what? They were absolutely right. Spending time with my loved ones with fun activities enhanced our relationships, promoted our understanding among each other, and built intimacy.

It took my husband and me five years to save enough money to bring our children to Walt Disney World. My husband drove our second-hand Dodge Caravan from Ontario, passing through Buffalo, New York, Ohio, West Virginia, South Carolina, Georgia, all the way to the sunny state of Florida. Thinking back, the car seemed so roomy, despite towing along baby clothes, diapers, and a stroller with our three little kids. And I couldn't help but laugh in the front seat as I heard my then-nine-year-old Ginny recite stories of Snow White, Cinderella, and the Muppet Babies to her sisters.

Since then, we've made similar road trips down south, each time returning with fond memories. But many things have changed throughout the years. For instance, we take turns driving. Philip is no longer the sole driver, as my two eldest daughters now volunteer to take over at the steering wheel. We also no longer need to carry bulky travel guides, brochures, and printed maps like 20 years ago. Now we use a small GPS that weighs less than eight ounces. As for that roomy feeling in the van … well, it's definitely gone, as six adults and piles of carry-on luggage, makeup bags, laptops, and trendy outfits have cramped the seats. Nursery rhymes and fairy tales are things of the past; now hip-hop music, Monopoly deals, and conversations about Harry Potter and Nintendo 3DS games fill the background noise. But one thing has remained unchanged: we always have our destination in mind, planning our stopover points and scheduling favorite activities along the way.

Fast Forward to Midlife Pondering

Watching my children grow in stature and wisdom challenges me to think about the next stage of my life. What will life look like when my children are grown and don't need me anymore? What do I do with the time I used to spend grocery shopping and cooking meals for four growing children? And what about the days I'm not mom chauffer, driving the kids to and from Kung Fu classes, piano lessons, school recitals, and friends' houses? Very soon, my husband and I will be able to go on vacation without worrying about our independent children. We won't need to take trips solely on long weekends, Christmas, or summer holidays. Finally, we can check out those off-peak, non-prime getaway deals. (How can anyone resist those $700 all-inclusive packages to Cuba?) Financially, we have our retirement funds and pensions set in relatively good order. Well, freedom 50-something is becoming a reality faster than I could imagine.

That said, what if every day was a no-obligation day in my retirement? No assignment deadlines, no boss to report to, no office hours to obey, no dress code to follow and, best of all, sleeping in every day without setting the alarm clock.

> ...what if every day was a no-obligation day in my retirement?

But then what? I could visit the places I always wanted to, meet with friends I haven't seen in awhile, take a yoga or tai-chi class, watch all the Korean drama DVDs I didn't have time to watch before. Or I could learn to play the piano and flute, or play golf, tennis, ski or swim. When I've had enough of those, I could throw in meaningful volunteer services, like reading to children at the library or serving meals to seniors at long-term care centers or retirement homes.

If you're enticed by these ideas, I challenge you to do them with strategic planning, so that these activities can fit into a bigger scheme that reflects you: a unique individual born with a special calling in life. I believe you can live a fulfilling and purposeful retirement. Let's pause and reflect on what retirement is all about.

Retirement Defined

In North America, retirement generally means that people leave their employment or occupation, withdrawing from an active working life. The most current statutory retirement age in Canada is 65; in the United States it is 67. Many people are looking into retiring earlier than that, especially those who are financially sound. On the other hand, some choose to work reduced hours yet keep their working role. Or they may start a part-time consulting career. Others may even postpone their retirement and continue working at their full capacity after they turn 65 or 67. Nonetheless, North American culture puts much emphasis on retirement financial planning. Many seminars, workshops, DVDs, books, and programs teach people how to invest wisely so that they can afford a desired lifestyle after they retire from the workplace.

I recognize the importance of financial planning—we need money to pay our mortgage, buy groceries, hire domestic help, and pay utility bills and medical insurance costs. Surely, having a sound financial plan or a big fat bank account is a helpful resource for anyone. However, this book will offer you significance beyond material means. It will help you develop an action plan that guides your retirement years to move your dreams forward, live life to its fullest, and leave a lasting legacy, all according to your unique life purpose. You may have already accomplished much, yet you can continue to make your contribution to society—somewhere now or in the long run. This requires deliberate soul-searching. You need to plan for success in this stage of life, as it's highly unlikely that it will happen by chance. Your life purpose remains to be discovered and developed. This is the essence of living life to its fullest.

The end of this chapter will help you consider some soul-searching questions and understand what retirement means to you. For now, let's go to the Bible and seek God's wisdom for His view on retirement.

What Does the Bible Say about Retirement?

According to *Statistics Canada*, women are expected to live to 83 years old, men about 78. I thought to myself, if I retire at 60, I have another 20-plus years to live. With mixed feelings about this, I immediately turned to the Bible and searched for retirement references for guidance. Based on my research and consultations with pastors, they have affirmed that the Bible has no direct reference to retirement or retirement planning, except for one passage in Numbers 8:23–26:

> *The LORD said to Moses, "This applies to the Levites: Men 20-five years old or more shall come to take part in the work at the tent of meeting, but at the age of fifty, they must retire from*

their regular service and work no longer. They may assist their brothers in performing their duties at the tent of meeting, but they themselves must not do the work. This, then, is how you are to assign the responsibilities of the Levites."

In this passage, the Lord instructs Moses to call upon all the Levite men between ages 25 and 49 to perform work on the tabernacle. Men over the age of 50 must not work like they used to. It is acceptable for these older men to provide assistance to the younger ones so that they can carry out their work duties at the tent. However, the older men must not perform the actual work.

Since this Bible passage is an account of what took place during Moses' leadership, what could be extracted here is a reference to that period of history rather than a universal rule. There is an age limit to work at the tent of meeting. This historical account is insufficient for anyone to derive a biblical principle around the concept of retirement.

On the other hand, we can see from the Bible that God called His servants to work laboriously into their old age. Moses started his ministry as the leader of Israel when he was 80 years old; he spent forty years leading the Israelites in the wilderness. Moses' career as a leader was at its height when God handed him the 10 Commandments at Mount Sinai when he was 80. His role continued until he passed away at the age of 120.[3]

God gave Abraham and Sarah their son Isaac when they reached old age. Abraham was 100 and Sarah was 90 when Isaac was born.[4] The prophet Samuel led Israel for 40 years. He passed on the torch to Saul and anointed Saul as the first king, when the Israelites wanted a king to rule over them instead of being led by a judge. Samuel obeyed God and served the people faithfully as prophet and judge from his youth until his death at an old age (according to some commentaries, Samuel lived to around 110).[5] Saul became king when he was 30 and he reigned for forty-two years until he was 72. David was the next king in Israel after Saul. Samuel also anointed David, and David reigned for forty years until he was 72.[6]

The Bible has numerous examples of people working continually through their lives, carrying specific roles. The concept of retirement is non-existent. Also, contrary to the idea of retirement, the Bible encourages us to proclaim God's wonderful deeds and power to the future generation, even during our golden years. The words of the psalmist echo this theme so eloquently:

As for me, I will always have hope;
I will praise you more and more.
Since my youth, God, you have taught me,
and to this day I declare your marvelous deeds.
Even when I am old and gray,
do not forsake me, my God,
till I declare your power to the next generation,
your mighty acts to all who are to come.
–Psalm 71:14, 17, 18

In the book of Isaiah, God affirms His love and care for His people from cradle to grave:

Listen to me, you descendants of Jacob,
all the remnant of the people of Israel,
you whom I have upheld since your birth,
and have carried since you were born.
Even to your old age and gray hairs
I am he, I am he who will sustain you.
I have made you and I will carry you;
I will sustain you and I will rescue you.
–Isaiah 46:3–4

May these passages encourage us to share God's supremacy and His wonderful deeds to our sons and daughters, nieces and nephews,

Sunday school children, or the young family residing next door to you.

Words of Wisdom

Knowing that God created us and promises to care for us into our old age, are there any reasons we would stop serving Him, thus retreating into an aimless life? Let me explain why I am asking this: I once heard a sermon by Dr. Tony Campolo, a sociology professor at Eastern University. What he shared was a profound insight and direction for the art of living. Dr. Campolo conducted a survey with 50 people over the age of 95. The survey asked the elderly what they would do differently if they could live their lives all over again. Out of all the different answers, these were the top results: a) they would risk more; b) they would reflect more; c) they would do more things that would live on after they passed away.[7]

The survey results do not point to anything about getting rich or having more material gains. The over-95-year-old survey participants remind us what really counts at the end of the day. It's not about owning a larger home or fancier car, or seeing all the wonders of the world. It is about doing something outside one's comfort zone, taking the time to think carefully, and leaving a legacy for future generations. What does it look like if we start embracing and incorporating their words of wisdom into our retirement plan?

Take More Risks

"Without risk, faith is an impossibility."
–Soren Kierkegaard (1813–1855), Danish philosopher, theologian, and religious author

When I used to play ping-pong, I had a friend who always told me to play it safe, reminding me not to risk the last two points since I would lead by 19–10. I should defend my 19-point score by keeping steady rather than smashing out for risky moves. The play-it-safe mentality is contrary to living a Christian life. We are called to put our trust in God. Putting our faith in things that can't be seen in the physical realm or in things yet to come is a risk. The Bible is filled with stories about risk-takers. And great things were accomplished through those brave men and women who were willing to risk their lives, fortune, and ambitions.

Timeless Heroes

The following is a brief review of three modern-day heroes: Mother Teresa, Dr. Viktor Frankl, and Rev. Billy Graham. Their tireless passions challenge us to see retirement differently.

Mother Teresa

Mother Teresa started her missionary journey when she was 18, to bring hope to the poor. She continued her passion as she grew older and was awarded the Nobel Peace Prize in 1979, accepting the award at age 69. Well into her 70s and 80s, Mother Teresa traveled across the world to continue caring for the poor through her foundation, *The Missionaries of Charity*.

Dr. Viktor Frankl

Dr. Viktor Frankl, a Holocaust survivor, was a prominent neurologist and psychiatrist. He continued to advance in his profession after his release from the Türkeim camp, and his lectures, books, and journal publications inspired many, even after his death at age 92. Age did not stop Frankl from accomplishing goals: he was a vigorous mountain climber and earned his pilot's license when he was 67. Until he was 85, Frankl taught at the University of Vienna.

Rev. Billy Graham

Rev. Billy Graham touched the hearts of many through his 70-plus years of ministry. He preaches all over the world and has authored more than 30 books, many of which have been translated into different languages. His autobiography, *Just As I Am*, took 10 years to complete and he finally finished the book at 78. Instead of dreading old age, his book encouraged readers to embrace this period, as God has lessons to teach us through this phase of life.

Abraham trusted God and took the leap of faith to leave his hometown, Ur, and settled in a foreign land in obedience to God's calling. A great nation came out of this man, who took the risk by faith.

In the New Testament, as recorded in Mark 10:17–22, a rich young man came to visit Jesus and inquired what he must do to inherit eternal life. Though he had obeyed all the commandments since he was a boy, he still lacked the one key thing that kept him from achieving his goal. Jesus loved him deeply and compassionately, and explained how the man needed to sell everything he had and give it to the poor. Subsequently, the man would be rich in heaven instead; then the man could come and follow Jesus, for He holds the key to eternal life. Unfortunately, this young man was not willing to risk his wealth, and he lost his claim to eternity.

Reflecting on our lives, did we pass an opportunity due to fear of the unknown, rejection, or failure? Do you dread going to work because you hate your job, yet you drag yourself to work day after day? The fear of failure or financial uncertainty can hold you back from acquiring a new skill, which could equip you to pursue a profession closer to your passion.

I remember when I had to choose between a promotion within a company I was working at as a full-time employee and a contract role that offered the prospect of being my own boss. Though the contract promised something I longed for—to be an entrepreneur and grow into uncharted territory, risks were involved. Without a steady flow of income from a company payroll, how could I ensure the bills got paid? Would I be able to land one contract after another to receive steady income? What if I became critically ill and needed short- or long-term disability benefits that aren't available for contractors? Leaving full-time employment also meant foregoing the prospect of climbing the corporate ladder, which could translate into higher paychecks, more enticing job titles, power, and a larger pool of subordinates. I chose to work as a freelance consultant, and I have not had a break in monthly income for more than six weeks in 10 years.

Are you holding on to the play-it-safe mindset when managing your relationships, work assignments, traveling, volunteering and such? Or are you prepared to take the leap of faith in exploring new possibilities: possibilities in making new friends, meeting new people, visiting different cultures, launching a second career or starting a new business venture, enjoying a new hobby, writing a book, or working in your dream job?

Reflections

Daily, I run on autopilot. Until recently, my routine went something like this: during the weekdays, I wake up at 6:20 AM, take a shower, apply my makeup; make coffee, pack my breakfast and lunch; wake up my son and drop him off at school; drink my coffee and eat my muffin in the car; drive another 40 kilometers to work. Then I stay in the office for at least eight hours; respond to my emails, return phone calls; check my to-do list, attend meetings, do some planning, prepare status reports, and resolve pressing issues. Before I know it, it's past 5 PM and I have to race home for another routine: make and eat dinner, wash dishes; do some reading, pray, and jot down a few lines in my prayer journal (that is, if I'm not too tired). Then, I collapse in my bed and the routine will start all over again the next day. You can probably substitute my routine with your day-to-day happenings. The details may be different, but the idea of running on autopilot is similar.

Our lives are often filled with modern-day busyness. How many times do we stop what we're doing, think about the implications and consequences, and intensely pay attention to details? Often times, the opposite is true. We take things we do for granted. "Oh, it's just another customer." "Hey, just another day wrapping up month-end processing." "If I can get through traffic and drop off my son faster, I can get to the office on time." Spending time in the car with our loved ones is a precious moment. The fact that we have a job in an uncertain economy is a blessing. Interacting with our colleagues is a blessing, too, since our behaviors reflect our faith. People see

Jesus through our deeds, our attitudes, what we say and don't say. Do we see these people as mere customers, colleagues, or subordinates? Or do we see them as lovely souls in need of Christ?

Through the hustle and bustle of daily living, do you ponder on the deeper meaning of life?

Where does your autopilot take you? Reflecting on what life is all about—for example, how we keep our relationships with loved ones and how we can make an impact at home, school, work, church, or community—will help shape our actions.

Through the hustle and bustle of daily living, do you ponder on the deeper meaning of life? Do you work to live or live to work? Take a pause; ask yourself what a spirit-filled life means to you while reviewing the following from Galatians 5:22–23:

> *But the fruit of the Spirit is love, joy, peace, forbearance, kindness, goodness, faithfulness, gentleness and self-control. Against such things there is no law.*

Beyond Profound Actions

Are you drawn to leaving a legacy of good fortune, positive deeds, ingenious inventions, or impacted lives? How are you planning to achieve these goals? You may have saved up a hefty retirement fund, a substantial life insurance policy and some other assets that your loved one will benefit from after you pass on. But how do you compare the importance of building character to building wealth? What determines your decisions in making life choices? It's not too late to start building a lasting legacy.

On the contrary, you may be struggling financially to provide for your family or to support yourself. You may suffer from ill health. You may worry about what the future holds for you in retirement years. God is faithful to carry you through difficult situations. My friend shared her story about how she had lost 80 percent of her modest savings due to the plunging stock market. Her hope of recovering this loss was dismal and yet, she did not place her hope in financial gain. She started to turn her attention to examining her life purpose. She devoted her time in crafting children's books to teach key virtues such as patience, faith, kindness, etc., through stories. Her dream was to publish her work one day. She felt the peace within, though her bleak financial outlook remained unchanged.

There are many ways we can proclaim God's might and power to another generation, regardless of your state of health or finance. It may involve speaking out for marginalized individuals or passing on your valuable experience by teaching Sunday school, mentoring young workers at organizations, encouraging your loved ones through prayers and kind words, or by writing a book or journal to record God's blessings in your life.

What's Next in Life?

> "I am always doing that which I cannot do, in order that I may learn how to do it."
> –Pablo Picasso (1881–1973), Spanish cubist painter

Now that we have reviewed the definition of retirement, visited the biblical concept of continuous service, and gained insight from others, ask yourself this: how do you want to spend your retirement years? Will it be filled with leisure living, traveling, or relaxing? Or will it be a journey that takes you to fulfill your unrealized dreams, to live out your purpose, passion, and potential?

The later chapters will take you to a strategic approach in planning your retirement. As you consider the meaning of retirement in your life, I invite you to pause and pray this prayer:

> Dear God,
> Thank you for assuring me that you care and watch over me, even when I become old and gray. You put

me on this earth for a special purpose, as you remind me that I am fearfully and wonderfully made. You know my strengths and weaknesses. You have counted the number of hairs on my head. You knew me before I was born. Nothing can be hidden from you.

You have seen my successes and failures. You also understand my hopes and dreams. You hold the keys to locked doors and you graciously open doors of opportunities for me. I want to commit the rest of my life in your hands as I look to the future, especially during my retirement years. I pray that you will guide me in discovering who I am and give me the wisdom to discern my calling. Out of your glorious riches, may you strengthen me through your spirit, so I can state your wondrous deeds and power to the next generation.

Amen

Take Action

Continue to pray as you review the following questions. You will have a chance to write what retirement means to you. Remember, we are serving a God with infinite wisdom; in Him, nothing is impossible. I challenge you to dream big dreams for your future. You are the only one who can carry out what God has designed for you. Capture your most candid responses to the following questions before turning to the next section. These responses will prepare you for Chapter 2, which will help you understand why planning works for your retirement.

1. Which of your pastimes bring glory to God's name?

2. What can you do to spread God's marvelous deeds and mighty power to the next generation?

3. What risks are you willing to take to fulfill God's calling?

4. What would you start doing if you could press the restart button on your life?

a. What would you stop doing if you could live life all over again?

b. What would you continue to do?

5. What is the meaning of retirement to you?

Summary

You've just reviewed the definition of retirement and how the Bible highlights lifelong service. You have gained insight from other words of wisdom and identified your personal view of retirement. You have also noted the need for planning to help you fulfill a purposeful life.

I trust that you're sitting comfortably in the driver's seat, anticipating what's next in your course of action. Yes, you will achieve greater things, move your dreams forward and live out a purposeful and fulfilling retirement. You are ready to take a strategic approach in planning your retirement beyond leisure living, traveling, and relaxing. I pray you will commit all that you do to the Lord, as He takes pleasure in blessing our plans in leaving a lasting legacy.

Only be careful, and watch yourselves closely so that you do not forget the things your eyes have seen or let them fade from your heart as long as you live. Teach them to your children and to their children after them.
–Deuteronomy 4:9

two

REDEFINE YOUR RETIREMENT

"I was young and now I am old,
yet I have never seen the righteous forsaken
or their children begging bread."
–Psalm 37:25

"We do not need magic to change the world.
We carry all the power we need inside ourselves already:
we have the power to imagine better."
–J.K. Rowling, British author

"We can recreate ourselves … in a different way than the
boundaries of our previous life allowed."
–Joan Chittister, author of *The Gift of Years: Growing Older Gracefully*

I HAVE NOT SEEN MY HIGH-SCHOOL ACQUAINTANCE, CARMEN, in almost 40 years. It's understandable since we've been living in different parts of the world. Carmen was the 'popular' girl in our teen years; she was captain of the school volleyball team and champion of the 100-metre and 200-metre track tournaments for four years. She won countless medals and awards in both intramural and citywide sports events. I admired Carmen's athletic and training persistence; but I, on the other hand, whipped up countless excuses for not attending gym class.

Thanks to social networking on the Internet, I reconnected with Carmen via Facebook and witnessed a profound video posted on her online profile. This time, she wasn't receiving a gold medal in a 400-metre race. Now, she was spirited and holding her head high in her navy blue-belted police uniform. In front of 100 admiring colleagues, she was being applauded and celebrated at her much-deserved retirement ceremony.

As I glued my eyes to this short video, I was in awe of how much this strong woman has achieved. Carmen, now a retired police inspector, spent 30 years working in the Royal Police Force in Hong Kong. At the mere age of 51, she was able to transition into a coveted retirement, relishing in exotic travels and part-time grandparental duties.

In Carmen's case, retirement has offered an exciting opportunity for freedom, especially for exploring new interests. Maybe you have a different perspective of what a dream retirement entails, be it traveling abroad, working part-time, volunteering, teaching, pursuing higher education, joining a quilting club, learning how to golf or curl, you name it. Understanding the principles behind the concept of retirement will open your mind to the possibilities ahead. In this chapter, we'll unpack the four realities of retirement, the kingdom view of retirement, and four interpretations on life stages.

The Realities of Retirement

Being aware of the faces of retirement prepares us for opportunities, constraints, uncertainties, risks, and options that may pop up in this life journey. As you review these points, highlight the information most relevant to you. Make note of arguments that resonate with your situations and follow up with the required actions; this will help you plan your retirement.

Reality #1: Retirement is not one-size-fits-all

There is no one-size-fits-all solution to living a purposeful and fulfilling retirement. Life is full of choices. You are the one who chooses how to retire and what to do during this time.

I consulted my financial advisor and asked her if I had enough money in my retirement fund if I were to, hypothetically speaking, retire next year. Her answer was politically correct: that is, she couldn't give me a straight answer! After sensing my confusion, she repeated the universal rule of thumb in generating retirement income: I need to generate 75 to 80 percent of my pre-retirement income during retirement to maintain my current lifestyle.

Why couldn't my financial advisor precisely answer a seemingly simple question? Well, there really isn't a standard retirement package, especially since everyone has a different lifestyle. Some may downsize, others may not; some may move back to their hometown or to another county with a different standard of living. Some may opt to work part-time to continue generating income. I've jotted down the factors that influence the retirement price tag:

1) Where do I want to retire?

I have a retired friend who sold her house in order to rent a small apartment. She would spend six months in Toronto, then six months in Florida. As you can see, you can choose to live anywhere you want during your retirement. Do I plan to stay in the city—where I am currently living—for the next decade? Do I want to move to the countryside or to an affordable suburb? I could even move to another province with a different climate and lifestyle. (Since I'm an immigrant from Hong Kong, China, I could move back there to join my old friends. Imagine the parties every week!) Or do I want to move into a retirement community, where assisted living is available?

2) What will I do after my retirement?

There are endless options here. I could live extravagantly, modestly, or somewhere in between. Some retirees sign up for golf memberships. Others make plans to travel to exotic places; they enjoy researching tourist attractions and historic facts before they set sail. Since I am not an adventurous traveler, I would probably keep my expenses to a minimum and watch my budget before making big purchases or committing to a travel plan. However, others may think differently and that is perfectly acceptable.

3) What income sources do I expect to have?

Do I plan to engage in income-generating activities or will I only rely on my savings and pension? It's possible for retirees or pensioners to go back to work and continue to earn an income. They can work full-time, part-time, or on a contract basis. In recent years, there has been an increasing trend for retirees to continue working in the same company or another company in a similar field. The Canadian Centre for Policy Alternatives has reported that a growing number of Canadians are continuing to work past age 65. In 2012, 24 percent of people aged 65 to 70 are still working compared to 11 percent in 2000, an increase of 13 percent in a decade.[8] According to Randstad's 2011 *Global Workmonitor* survey, 70 percent of employees in India, Mexico, Singapore and the U.S. anticipate working beyond their official retirement age. In particular, 52 percent of Canadians see themselves working beyond age 65; almost half are content to continue working two years after their retirement.[9]

Since retirees usually have many years of valuable experience and expertise, they can become consultants or advisors, boosting the organizational talent pool. A 2012 survey by Sun Life Financial Canada revealed that 48 percent of Canadians plan to work part-time or freelance while they ease into retirement.[10]

If a retiree has other interests not fully developed due to circumstantial constraints, retirement is convenient for acquiring new skills through re-training. A retiree—sometimes called a mature worker—could enter a new profession altogether and find fulfillment in a new line of work. Cindy, the baby boomer role model you'll meet in chapter four, is a prime example in this regard.

Reality #2: There are positive and negative associations to retirement

We have a biological clock ticking away. We grow older by the minute while we celebrate our birthday year after year. But in North America, our culture tends to glorify youth, embrace physical beauty, and equate growing old to something that should be masked or avoided. Are we driven by fear and denial as we confront the quick disappearing of our youthful looks? Do we anticipate the annoyances of increased aches and pain, the gradual diminishment of our physical and mental capabilities, and the threat of greater isolation?

The retirement phase brings us closer to our final passage: death. Does facing your mortality bring on feelings of doom and gloom? Are there any positive perspectives? Some deeper introspection can help us appreciate the storehouse of knowledge and wisdom we've accumulated over the years. We can look forward to passing down our knowledge, gifts, and experiences to subsequent generations.

In her book, *The Gift of Year: Growing Older Gracefully*, author Joan Chittister encourages readers to accept and celebrate growing old. There is much to cherish, because aging is a natural part of life that is active, productive, and intensely rewarding. She argues that this last period of human growth "can be lived as a summit-time of life." This awareness promotes our commitment to finding the beauty of aging.[11] (On a side note, Joan was 70 years old when she wrote her book, and, not only that, she still thought of herself as young!)

Reality #3: Retirement can be voluntary, involuntary, or delayed

Some choose to retire and others retire due to circumstantial factors. It's important to acknowledge this fact to prepare for the unexpected.

Voluntary Retirement

Some people willfully retire from their active working life, such as my high-school friend Carmen. They may have achieved their career goals and they do not need to rely on income from regular employment or paid assignments. Or they're financially adequate and don't need to work.

Involuntary Retirement

Others are forced into retirement due to situations beyond their control (such as layoffs or mandatory retirement). During the global economic downturn of 2007, many lost their jobs and were unable to find meaningful employment that matched their skillsets or career aspirations. There were disheartening stories from many middle-aged people who were seeking work for months, even years, and had no luck landing jobs. They eventually gave up looking for work altogether.

Delayed retirement

In Canada, the law that stipulates mandatory retirement at age 65 for federally regulated employees was repealed as of December 2012. Most provinces have eliminated mandatory retirement at this traditional age. At the same time, recent changes to the Canada Pension Plan (CPP) have made early retirement less attractive, while there are increased incentives for delaying it. For example, those waiting until age 70 to receive their CPP will get 42 percent more than if CPP were taken at 65.

...more people beyond the age of 65 are remaining in the workforce, so delayed retirement is a new trend.

As mentioned earlier, more people beyond the age of 65 are remaining in the workforce, so delayed retirement is a new trend. The *Financial Post* summarized two major factors behind this movement: some are forced to work because big chunks of their savings were wiped out in the stock market turmoil in recent years. Others have skills that are in demand, as companies require talent from mature workers to strengthen the relatively inexperienced workforce.[12]

Reality #4: Retirement requires financial support for an unknown time

When a person retires, it may mean they no longer have income or that income reduces drastically. A few common sources of funds are available for most retirees to draw from: a personal retirement savings plan, private investments, and personal assets such as real estate, company pension or government pension, and old age security programs. Sometimes a company pension plan provides a steady income stream to employees after they've reached a certain age and after they stop working.

In Canada, Canadian citizens are entitled to collect CPP starting at age 65. The amount of CPP benefit depends on the contribution level of the individual in earlier years. As of 2012, the maximum amount of CPP Canadians can collect is $986 per month. This amount is adjusted every January based on the cost of living, as measured by the Consumer Price Index (CPI). Some Canadian retirees can also benefit from Old Age Security (OAS) and Guaranteed Income Supplement (GIS) if they are eligible. The maximum benefits for OAS and GIS are $540 and $732 respectively.[13] So for individuals who formerly earned $50,000 annually, relying on the Canadian social system actually meets less than half of their pre-retirement income.

The amount of money needed to support our retirement lifestyle, travels, leisure activities, health-care expenses and other expenditures varies based on personal preference and needs. In reality, we need financial support for as long as we live. As I conducted a casual round of statistics on my own family, the numbers are impressive. My father lived to 79. My mom is 82 and going strong. My father-in-law lived to 76. My mother-in-law is 88 years old and she lives independently, plus manages her three-bedroom detached home immaculately! My husband's grandmother was 96 years old when she passed away. Noticeably, we commonly see older, active seniors around. It reminds me to put more money aside for the long haul.

Regrettably, other factors add to financial uncertainty. Just like their international neighbors, Canadians are confronting a collapsing financial market, rising commodity prices, a draining tax system, expensive health-care costs, and despicable savings rates. Baby boomers entering the traditional retirement age are struggling to cope with the harsh realities of limited social support, plus a pessimistic outlook of the global economy.

Being informed and managing our retirement assets are definite to-dos for surviving the long haul. Life is full of challenges—our worries will not help diminish the risks. Rather, faith can carry us through uncertainties and keep us above the storm. There is a bright side to the future besides the doom and gloom. Not all of us have a seven-digit retirement savings account. You may be forced into retirement due to a layoff. Or you may have to deal with financial commitments such as mortgages. We can do our part to learn how to manage our assets wisely and counter the unknown with faith.

The Kingdom View

The Bible has many references that address the attitude of wealth. From the Old Testament, we have seen many demonstrations of prosperous individuals who trust and fear God. Abraham is a suitable example, as he owned precious metals, livestock, and commodities. Despite his impressive assets, Abraham is known for his faith in God rather than his material possessions. However, if you follow the Book of Genesis, you'll notice a recurring theme of God blessing those who have faith in Him, even into their old age.

Abraham was now old and well advanced in years,
and the LORD had blessed him in every way.
–Genesis 24:1

Another example is the famous King Solomon. We can achieve a purposeful and fulfilling retirement by gleaning from Solomon's wisdom. In his book, *The Richest Man Who Ever Lived: King Solomon's*

Secrets to Success, Wealth, and Happiness, author Steven Scott describes a personal breakthrough in his success story.[14] Scott rolled from one job to the next for six years after completing college. Deciding to turn a new page at his friend's suggestion, Scott began studying a chapter of Proverbs every day. Two years later, his small partnership business thrived into a multi-million-dollar enterprise. So what does King Solomon's secret to success, wealth, and happiness have to do with us?

As recorded in the Old Testament, shortly before David's death, Solomon was 12 years old when he was installed as king. God appeared to Solomon in a dream, asking him which wish he wanted to be granted.[15] Solomon recognized that it was a huge undertaking to be ruler of the great nation of Israel. His request was to have wisdom and knowledge to carry out his daunting duty.

God's answer to Solomon was remarkable. Solomon did not ask for long life, riches, honor, or victory over his enemies; rather, he requested wisdom and knowledge, so God granted Solomon what he asked. God also gave the young leader the items he did not ask for: riches and honor. Thus, Solomon's riches were unprecedented and unmatchable compared to former and future kings.

The Bible has at least 250 verses that discuss money. Jesus makes His point clear in Matthew 6, stating how we should not store treasure on this earth, yet store treasures in heaven instead: *"For where your treasure is, there your heart will be also"* (Matthew 6:21). Jesus further warns us how no one can serve God and money concurrently, since the love of money will draw away our focus and attention from following God.

However, there is a dilemma here. Financial experts stress the need to save a sizeable amount of retirement savings because the social safety net is gone, the global economy is on the verge of collapse, and interest rates are at a pitifully low level. However, God's view is extremely different yet assuring. He gently whispers and invites us to trust Him and He will provide all that we need. *"But seek first his kingdom and his righteousness, and all these things will be given to you as well"* (Matthew 6:33).

In regards to making use of God's gifts, Jesus teaches His disciples to invest wisely in the story about investment.[16] In this parable, the servants—who invested the money their master had given them—received double the original amount. Their master commended them: *"Well done, good and faithful servant! You have been faithful with a few things; I will put you in charge of many things. Come and share your master's happiness"* (Matthew 25:21). The servant who did not seek an investment opportunity and hid the money in the ground was harshly reprimanded by the master: *"You wicked, lazy servant"* (Matthew 25:26).

Summing up from the accounts of Abraham, King Solomon, and Jesus' teachings on money, these are four lessons for us on adopting the right attitudes when handling money:

1. ***God recognizes that we need money to live.*** We should continue working hard to make a living using our talents and skills to support our families and ourselves.

2. ***Being wealthy is not a sin.*** In the Bible, God has indeed blessed many wealthy individuals. There are also many millionaires today who live by the faith and follow the precepts taught in the Bible.

3. ***We should be good stewards of our money.*** God expects us to handle our money diligently by investing carefully and wisely.

4. ***We should be generous in giving***. God is the source of all wealth and He holds the vastness of the universe. The material riches we enjoy today are blessings that outflow from the supreme source.

I have no need of a bull from your stall or of goats from your pens, for every animal of the forest is mine, and the cattle on a thousand hills.
–Psalm 50:9–10

Some trust in chariots and some in horses, but we trust in the name of the LORD our God.
–Psalm 20:7

So far, we have carefully considered the broad realities of retirement, gleaning at godly attitudes towards wealth. Now, let's approach retirement in light of the various life stages. It's important to acknowledge the characteristics of these stages and note the growth opportunities with each stage. This awareness will guide you to climb new heights during your retirement, allowing you to capitalize on everything you've experienced in your previous life stages.

Understanding Life Stages

In the human life cycle, the different stages of development are usually marked as newborn to teenager, teenager to adolescence, adolescence to adult, and adult to old age. I will take you through the characteristics and typical activities of each stage, identifying opportunities during the retirement period.

The Two Halves of Life

For those of us who have lived for more than four or five decades, if we simply look at life as two halves—life before 50 and life after 50, which half do you think is beter?

Two Halves of Life

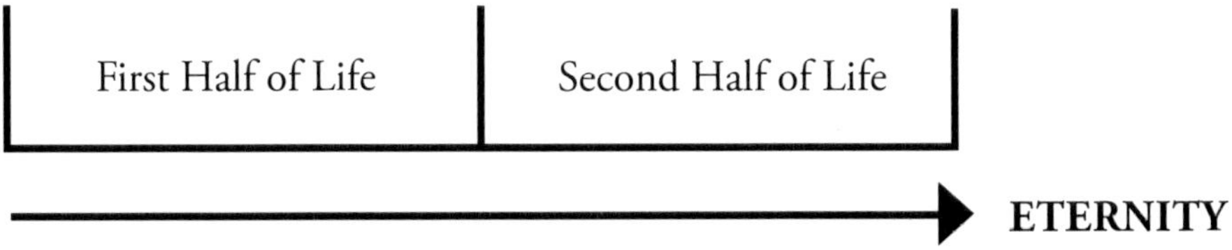

As I enter my own second half of life, I'm very excited about the future. I have an overwhelming sense of freedom since I am no longer bound by other people's opinions. After many trials and errors, I know exactly what I want in life. For years, my life has been about obtaining academic credentials, building a career, raising my children, attending to family responsibilities, caring for elderly parents, studying to keep up with skills required at work, paying off the mortgage, car loan and life insurance premiums, saving money for rainy days, responding to requests to serve at church … the list goes on. Just writing it down tires me out! Your case may be similar or far more challenging. Have you ever wondered how you've made it this far?

David Niven, Ph.D., best-selling author of *The 100 Simple Secrets of the Best Half of Life: Make Your Second Half the Best Half*, reviewed more than a thousand scientific studies on the second half of life. He further filtered these findings and boiled down to 100 essential ways for finding (and maintaining) daily happiness, health, and satisfaction. The common themes from those essentials include the importance of attitudes, perspectives, and a willingness to act.[17] Accordingly, we can live contently and maintain vitality every day by adopting these helpful strategies.

Mature Matters

My friend Audrey recently commented on the phrase empty nest. She realized she hadn't had a decent meal with her husband for over 20 years. When her children were younger, she or her husband would rush home after work, cook dinner, and help the children with their homework. The other parent would work overtime, then go grocery shopping to prepare for the next day. When the children became teenagers, the schedules became more chaotic! It was often a medley of fast food or quick dinners with piano lessons, hockey practices, and dance recitals in between. It was only last year, after their youngest son went off to university, that Audrey and her husband finally had a quiet meal together. What a strange yet refreshing feeling!

Furthermore, Audrey started a new career in her early 50s as a registered nurse. She currently works 12-hour shifts in a psychiatric hospital. Her empty-nest journey is a firm reminder of Dr. Gene Cohen's book, *The Mature Mind*. Dr. Cohen hypothesizes four phases of psychological development in a maturing life: re-evaluation, liberation, summing up, and encore.[18]

Re-evaluation

Audrey went through a period of soul-searching in her middle age and decided to further her studies in nursing—despite the fact she already earned her Bachelor of Science and MBA degrees. In Cohen's terms, Audrey re-evaluated her aspirations. The re-evaluation phase is about exploration and transition. Dr. Cohen argues that at roughly ages 40 to 65, we have the desire to reflect on where we've been and where we're going. Most people seek for truth and significance and for what is most meaningful in their lives. I was at this place when I had the urge to work on my life mission statement a few years ago. (You'll have a chance to read about my self-discovery in Part II.)

Liberation

According to Cohen, the liberation phase consists of innovation and experimentation. By the time we reach our late 50s, 60s and into the 70s, we have gained significant life experiences. The brain's ability to make new connections between brain cells enables us to utilize both the right- and left-brain hemispheres more efficiently. The powerful potential of the brain actually enhances—rather than diminishes—our lives after age 50. We are free to create and turn ideas into new possibilities.

My former pastor is a great example of liberating into new realms following retirement. Rev. Dr. Daniel Ng, a retired pastor from the Hamilton Chinese Alliance Church (HCAC), served as senior pastor at HCAC for 32 years prior to his retirement in his late 60s. Not long after his official retirement, Rev. Ng took up an interim pastor role for another church and he served there for four years. He currently leads short-term mission trips to South American countries regularly. Rev. Ng has a heart for missions and mentorship. Whenever his schedule permits, he provides guidance to a group of church leaders, preaches, and teaches at conferences. Rev. Ng is sharp, passionate, active, vibrant, dynamic, and full of life, even into his 70s!

Summing Up

Dr. Cohen suggests that the summing-up phase is about resolution and review. In our late 60s, through the 70s and well into the 80s, we recap past life events. It's common to feel the desire to give back to society, enriching our families and friends through service or volunteerism. I can relate this phase to many seniors, including my mother-in-law and her readiness to contribute. My mother-in-law always looks for opportunities to bless her children and grandchildren. When she was in her 60s, she helped my husband and me raise our four children. My husband and I were so busy with work, sometimes we couldn't come home until midnight. She would take care of the household chores and care for the little ones tenderly and patiently. Up to a couple of years ago, in her 80s, she was still cooking our favorite dishes for special occasions. She would fervently plan the menu, visit the stores multiple times to select the right ingredients, carefully sort the meat and vegetables, cutting them for presentation, prepare the ingredients in her homemade sauce, and then hand-package them so that each family member would receive a portion of that exceptional dish.

Encore

This phase generally starts during our late 70s, extending to the end of a lifetime. The encore phase consists of repeating or continuing to celebrate love and companionship and giving back to society. When a person comes to an extremely old age, there is a desire to remain vital in the face of difficult circumstances. This is the will to live, which keeps us going strong and creative. For example, my dad demonstrated resilience and a robust desire to maintain his physique into his late 70s. He would join my family for bike rides and walk around the track in the local schoolyard. He always found ways to keep his mind alert, despite being alone during the day. I found my dad doing four activities regularly: walking and stretching, reading books, practicing calligraphy, and playing chess. When no one was around, he played chess with both hands. His left hand was his opponent. At age 79, he was sent to the hospital for heart surgery. He assured us he had a good life and would love to be around for a few more years to see my brother get married. He remained resilient and innovative until his passing.

> ...the brain continues to flourish rather than weaken in the second half of life.

Understanding these phases and the underlying mechanism at work brings motivation, energy, direction, and a sense of purpose. This means your creativity and intellect remains strong as you age, and you still have the ability to enjoy satisfying relationships. Dr. Cohen's research suggests there are surprising positive changes in life over the age of 50; for that reason, the brain continues to flourish rather than weaken in the second half of life.

The Three Stages of Life

In early 2012, the Canadian government announced the plan to increase the age of eligibility for Old Age Security (OAS) benefits from 65 years old to 67. Traditionally, we have been under the mindset that people go through life in three major stages: from childhood to adolescence, young adulthood to middle age, and then late adulthood to old age. Most people plan to work until they reach 60 or 65, and then they officially retire, start collecting pension, and enter a period of leisure living. Life in three stages looks like this:

Three Stages of Life

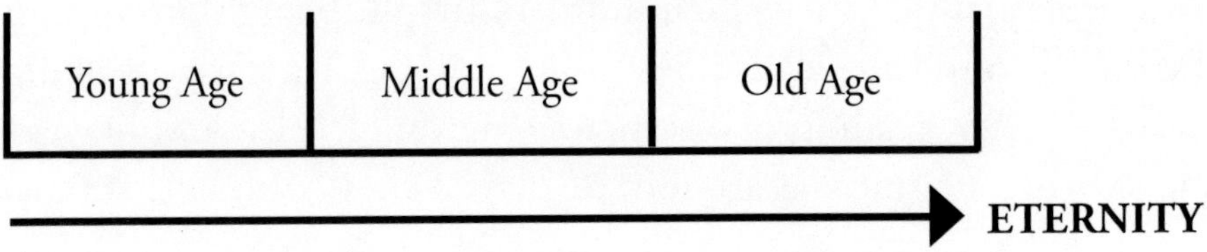

The characteristics of each stage are as follows:

Young Age (childhood to adolescence)

- Rapid development and growth
- Studying/schooling is the primary activity for at least 12, 15, or 20 years
- Dependence on family and social structure (societal systems and institutions such as schools, churches, and community support infrastructures)
- Development is an upward climb, an expansion into better capabilities such as life skills, language/literacy skills, and physical strength.

Middle Age (young adulthood to middle age)

- Productivity (i.e. building a career, raising a family)
- Achievement (i.e. obtaining professional qualifications, earning a promotion, contributing to society and community)
- Accumulation (i.e. building wealth, car or house ownership)
- Midlife crisis (i.e. reflecting on the prospect of fleeting youth, the meaning of life, what has already been achieved and what is to come)

- Development steadily rising with the prospect of building better capabilities

Old Age (late adulthood to old age)

- Leisure (i.e. disengaging from an active work life)
- Withdrawal (i.e. diminishing social connectedness)
- Decline (i.e. over the hill, out to pasture, twilight years)
- Questioning (i.e. what do we do with all we've gathered or accumulated?)
- Deep reflection (i.e. evaluating everything we have come to know about life)
- Seeking (i.e. meaning of life, legacy for the future generation)
- Development is no longer an upward climb; rather it is believed to be 'over the hill'

In a traditional sense, the stages are treated as three distinct boxes, where the major activities of each stage do not cross over to the next.

The Three Boxes of Life

In his book, *The Three Boxes of Life and How to Get Out of Them*, author Richard N. Bolles demonstrated the negative implications of defining our lifespan into three rigid periods. These periods are based on education, work, and retirement. Many people experience each box-like stage, said Bolles, and therefore do little other than the primary activities of schooling, employment, and stepping down from paid work into leisure.[19]

Bolles' unflavored three boxes are parallel to the conventional view of retirement from the past few decades. After most workers spent 30 or 40 years in intense labor or office work, they naturally retreated into a brief period of disengagement and leisure. Early in my career, for instance, I witnessed a few celebrations that sent off long-term employees to their happy retirement. In 1989, my ex-boss Jack had worked for a medium-size Canadian manufacturing company since his early 30s. He was the youngest accountant when he started with the company, and was eventually promoted to controller and then vice-president of finance. On his 65th birthday, the company held a party for Jack, which was also a fond farewell from the workforce. Jack was proudly entering his 'freedom years.' To commemorate his years of hard work, the company awarded Jack a six-foot-tall antique grandfather clock, a Compaq Portable 386 computer, a Nikon camera, and a beautiful oil painting.

The Education box in Bolles' illustration denotes a period of physical growth, preparation, and learning. From childhood to their late teens or into their early 20s, people would study, learn a trade, obtain a degree, help out on the farm, learn the essential life skills and so forth.

At around age 20 or a little older, people then engage in work-related activities, such as landing a job in an auto factory, a bank, a government agency, or some other organization. This Work box denotes a period of career building, active employment, professional activities, homemaking and such. This is a time for productivity, achievements, and responsibilities. People could stay in this box for most of their working lives before their employers handed over retirement packages and thanked them for their long-term contribution, very similar to Jack's situation.

The Retirement box—which usually occurs between ages 50 and

68—denotes a period of leaving active employment, disengaging from social duties, and retreating to a life of leisure. Back in the 1900s, the life expectancy for American men was about 47 years, 50 for women. Retirement for people in the early 20th century entailed a brief period of leisure living. As the life expectancy increased by about 50 percent over the last 100 years in the U.S., the Retirement box can stretch out to a period of 10 or more years.

Bolles encourages readers to strike an optimal balance between learning, working, and playing (leisure); therefore, we should design a plan to blend in the primary activities from each of these three periods. Rather than remain boxed in, make it a continuous journey that leads to the fulfillment of life meaning and purpose. The traditional paradigm of study/career/leisure can be enhanced to include a deliberate approach to life planning. Striking a balance, along with a smooth transition from one box to the next, depends heavily on what you want in life.

From my own experience, I agree with Bolles' view on life planning. Discovering your life purpose is the basis for defining what you want. Once you figure this out, implementing what you want will involve balancing activities in each phase. Accordingly, you'll need to manage the transitions that lead to fulfilling your life purpose.

The Third Age

Peter Laslett (1915–2001) was a demographic historian, sociologist, and authoritative activist on aging in Great Britain. In his book, *A Fresh Map of Life: The Emergence of the Third Age,* Laslett redefined the traditional view of life stages from three to four, coining it the Four Ages of Life.[20] Laslett sketched the Third Age, arguing that the crown of life should be pursued when work responsibilities are over and the children are grown. Each age is marked by key characteristics:

- *The First Age* marks the period of childhood dependency and socialization.

- *The Second Age* marks the period of responsibility and work life.
- *The Third Age* marks the period of personal fulfillment and achievement. (This age marks the culmination of all life stages.)
- *The Fourth Age* marks the period of dependency and frailty.

These ages do not stretch out to a number of exclusive years. It is possible to live out the Third Age simultaneously with the Second Age. Passage from one to the next does not need to occur. Some people could live out the Third Age alongside the Second, enjoying the apogee of personal life while raising a family, building a career, and accumulating wealth. According to Laslett, the Third Age is a major part of the life cycle for many people. Instead of facing the retirement years as a period of declining health, inactivity, and feebleness, this period can include voluntary activities, freedom to explore other interests, and continuous growth. For the baby boomer or later generations, the four ages can be translated into the four key periods of life.

Instead of facing the retirement years as a period of declining health, inactivity, and feebleness, this period can include voluntary activities, freedom to explore other interests, and continuous growth.

When I map out the life stages of today's baby boomers or the middle-aged—who are expected to live actively and independently well into their 90s—this is what it looks like:

Four Stages for Baby Boomers or the Middle-Aged

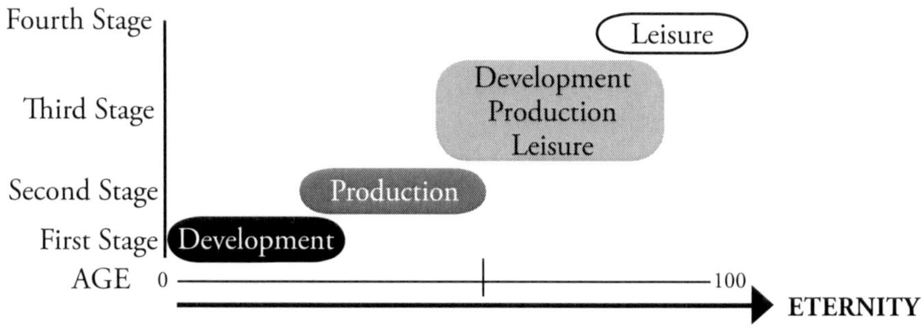

Take a closer look and you'll notice how these four stages are not in boxes, nor are they disconnected from the previous stage. The stages overlap. Some people can continue to build a career (in the Production stage) and study at the same time (in the Development stage). Looking back at your own life, can you relate to these four stages?

The *First Stage* consists of growth and development. The primary activities during these first 20-something years are education, preparing for a career, and transitioning into independence.

The *Second Stage* is a time for enhancing productivity, which may include building a career, working for an income, raising a family, etc.; tangible outcomes such as these are the primary themes of this stage.

The *Third Stage* is where Development, Production, and Leisure co-exist and materialize simultaneously. This is significant—we need to think about continuous learning (Development), lifelong service (Production), and engaging in activities that bring us joy (Leisure). These undertakings fuel each other, enriching and enlightening us while keeping the creative juices flowing. (Note: The next chapter is devoted to insights and strategies that enable us to extend this stage and age gracefully. This book is about living this stage of life with passion, purpose, and fulfillment.)

The *Fourth Stage* is the final period, where a person disengages in worldly responsibilities and enters the passage to the end of life. Development and productivity is no longer the primary focus because the decline of physical and mental abilities sets in.

Next, I mapped out each decade by their characteristics, key activities, and any social markers that associate with the corresponding age range. The New-Old Paradigm for this generation of retirees may look like the following chart:

The New-Old Paradigm

Approx. Age	Typical Characteristic	Typical Key Activity	Typical Social Marker
0 to 10	Growth Development	Play Learn Character shaping Experimentation Education	Dependent on family
11 to 20	Development Preparation		Dependent on family and social structure (i.e. schools, churches, community organizations, etc.)
21 to 30	Establishment Development Production Building Achievement	Experimentation Obtaining credentials and/or professional certification Getting married Buying a car Owning a house Starting a business Building a career Forming a family Extending territory Raising children	Being independent or married; having children, social connectedness (affinity groups)
31 to 40			
41 to 50			Midlife crisis
51 to 60	Stability Development Production Achievement	Continuous education Accumulating wealth and knowledge Starting a new career Enjoying freedom to explore new interests	Leisure Giving back to society
61 to 70			

71 to 80	Stability Maturity Wisdom	Freedom to explore new interests	Retirement Leisure Disengagement
81 to 90		Gradual decline in activity level	
91 to 100+	Decline in physical capabilities	Limited mobility	Diminish social connectedness

The New-Old Paradigm chart depicts a breakdown of typical characteristics, key activities, and social markers by each decade. This chart is provided to stretch your imagination to the opportunities that lie ahead. However, depending on your health and personal circumstances, the chronological ages may not always align to the corresponding characteristics, activities, or social markers.

Now I invite you to re-imagine the word retirement and answer the following review questions. Listen to yourself as you reflect on each question—allow your intuition to take control. Your answers will help your future planning. Tick off the appropriate answer or expand if the question calls for it.

Review Questions

1. What would you call your new stage of life? You can check off the most appealing choice from the list or fill in your own name for it in the blank line.

   - ❑ Crown of Life
   - ❑ Summit of Life
   - ❑ Better Half of Life
   - ❑ Freedom Years
   - ❑ Golden Years
   - ❑ Bonus Years

❑ The Rest-of-Life
❑ Second Adulthood
❑ Second Adolescence
❑ Un-retirement
❑ Renewment
❑ ____________________

2. At what age do you plan to retire?

3. How do you plan to retire?
   ❑ Never retire (continue working for as long as I am able)
   ❑ Partially retire (work part-time or take a short retirement, then return to work)
   ❑ Fully retire (disengage from an active working life)
   ❑ Retire and re-invent (go back to school and/or start another career)

4. What key activities do you see yourself involved in during your retirement?

5. Where do you want to live when you retire?

Summary

The four realities of retirement have been outlined, which will help you to be flexible, realistic, and proactive while facing the prospect of retiring. You have also visited the Bible's view on wealth and evaluated the four life stages. Does the next phase of your life intrigue or excite you? Maybe you already have a grand scheme halfway launched. In the next chapter, you'll look at a vast reservoir of resources within you, which will help you gain insight into aging gracefully.

"Finishing life for the glory of Christ."
–John Piper, pastor, author of *Rethinking Retirement*

"Life is about becoming more than we are, about being all that we can be."
–Joan Chittister, author of *The Gift of Years: Growing Older Gracefully*

Part Two

LIVING YOUR BEST

Don't settle for second-best. Living your best at different stages of life requires intention and determination, partnered with helpful strategies and winning attitudes. Know the facts and plan for the long haul.

three

AGING GRACEFULLY IN BODY, MIND, AND SPIRIT

*"Listen to your father, who gave you life,
and do not despise your mother when she is old."*
–Proverbs 23:22

"It`s not how old you are, it`s how you are old."
–Jules Renard, (1864–1910), French writer

"Every child is an artist. The problem is how to remain an artist once he grows up."
–Pablo Picasso (1881–1973), Spanish cubist painter

OLD AGE IS RELATIVE. A 10-YEAR-OLD MAY THINK HER 16-YEAR-OLD sister is old. A 17-year-old boy might say his 27-year-old teacher is old. My retired baby-boomer friend volunteers at a retirement home and claims she serves the 'old folks' there.

Looking back to the early 1900s—when the average lifespan in the Western world was 47—very few people lived to see their grandchildren grow up. Fast-forward a century later and you'll notice how 30 years were added to people's lifespan. In 2010, the life expectancy for Canadians was reported to be over 80 and over 78 for Americans. Nowadays, the prevalence of four-generation families is not uncommon. For instance, my 84-year-old aunt lives in California and regularly enjoys visits from her four great-grandchildren; the oldest among them is 19 years old.

The concept of the old-old age versus the new-old age exists. My own grandparents (whom I never met) remind me of the old-old. My grandpa was not educated; he worked hard as a carpenter most of his life and into his early 50s. He became frail and died of an acute illness within 24 hours.

On the other hand, my late uncle exemplified the new-old. Uncle Wah, a hard-working, well-respected man who lived the American dream, finishing his earthly journey at the age of 83. Uncle Wah started working as a chef in California when he was 20 and later became a restaurant-owner. After 25 years of working in a thriving operation, he sold his restaurant and retired at 65 in 1994. He remained healthy and active after his retirement, traveling and visiting his families overseas. He cooked scrumptious roast beef dinners for special gatherings, engaged in community events, continued driving, and took short road trips to the very end.

Similar to my uncle, today's boomers or "seniors" are leading the new-old revolution—they stay independent, intellectually challenged, physically fit, and socially engaged and do most of the things they did when they were in their 40s. They're growing old yet staying young. But wait, is this really possible? When does that unpleasant reference to aging kick in?

In today's society, 50 is the magic age at which happiness seems to fall downhill, be it through your physical stamina, waistline, sex life, you name it. Other negative stereotypes of adults over 50 include being inflexible, unproductive, stubborn, boring, slow, and difficult. How are we responding to these stereotypes, especially those of us who are living past 50? An American study with three different age groups—middle-aged (45–64), young-old (65–74) and oldest-old (75 and older)—revealed that "the oldest cope at least as effectively as their younger counterparts, despite their likelihood of encountering increased levels of stress…" reported *The Journal of Genetic Psychology.*[21]

We can have a bright future that surpasses negative stereotypes on aging. Studies on aging and testimonies from the elderly have further confirmed the notion of living an abundant life—without an expiration date. The potential to maintain optimum strength physically and mentally later in life is supported by many research findings. This is also consistent with the biblical view of lifelong service and longevity.

Studies on aging and testimonies from the elderly have further confirmed the notion of living an abundant life —without an expiration date.

Hence, this chapter shatters the most common myths about aging. We will focus on:

Myth #1: An old brain can't learn new information

Wherein intellectual ability reaches its peak in the late teens or early 20s and declines thereafter.

Myth #2: Nature dictates how well we age

Your genes determine how fast you age. There is little you can do to alter that.

Myth #3: It's too late for "old" people to change

You can't do much to improve your quality of life. Damages are done and they can't be reversed.

We hear these myths often, yet they clash with scientific research. Researchers have learned that stressors, diseases, injuries, and lifestyles—rather than the aging process itself—trigger many of the negative changes behind aging. Really, you and I have total control over the choices we make today. Debunking aging myths will provide us with insights and strategies for making use of our innate abilities. This will enable us to age gracefully in body, mind, and spirit—now and into late adulthood.

Debunking Myth #1: An old brain can't learn new information

Studies have proven conventional wisdom to be wrong about intellectual ability reaching its peak in the late teens or early 20s. According to research by Drs. John W. Rowe and Robert L. Kahn of the MacArthur Foundation Study of Aging in America, "older people can recall and recognize [previous information and/or images] as well as young people."[22]

Dementia is not a normal sign of aging, though Alzheimer's disease affects about nine percent of people over 65 in Canada[23] and 13 percent of people over age 65 in the United States.[24] Age-related declines in cognitive function are most common in two areas: the speed of information processing and explicit memory, which is the ability to recall a certain name, place, object and such. Other types of memory show very little debility with age. The good news is that these declines rarely affect all types of cognitive performance; most of the losses come later in life.

Since ample brain and mind research supports the positive aspects of aging, I am devoting the next section to our aging brain. This awareness will help us appreciate our potential to excel in the coming years.

What is Intelligence?

"In youth we learn; in age we understand."
–Marie von Ebner Eschenbach (1830–1916), Austrian writer

When we think of intelligent people, we consider those who are sharp, quick, efficient, and analytical, with the ability to learn and process information rapidly. The American Psychological Association defines intelligence in a broader view, focusing less on the speed of processing information. Rather, the Association says intelligence is an individual's ability to comprehend complex ideas, surpass challenges through critical reasoning, and adapt to different environments effectively, based on previous experience.[25]

From this definition, it's important to note that intelligence goes beyond a high IQ and superior academic standings. This assertion supports findings that say older people do not lose their mental ability. Actually, the years of experience and adaptations to various environments and situations can expand—rather than reduce—the level of intelligence in the older population.

Reviewing intelligence that relates to our mental capability will help us take advantage of such phenomena. Let's consider four different theories on intelligence: fluid, crystallized, experiential, and emotional.

Fluid Intelligence

Fluid intelligence relates to the ability and speed of processing new information based on perceptual skills—the ability to analyze, interpret and give meaning to what is seen—and memory. It involves thinking and reasoning abstractly, such as the act of solving a crossword puzzle. Studies have shown that fluid intelligence is most affected by an older nervous system; in other words, the decline of fluid intelligence may start in middle age, more sharply into late adulthood. This observation supports the fact that older people exhibit slower mental reactions and are often less efficient in processing new information.[26]

Crystallized Intelligence

Crystallized intelligence is the ability to use accumulated knowledge to make judgments and solve problems; for example, a physician needs to use his medical knowledge and his patient's test results to make a diagnosis. As a person becomes enriched with new experiences and social interactions, crystallized intelligence actually increases, improving as we age. Studies have shown that crystallized intelligence continues to develop during early and late adulthood.[27]

A look into the life of Mayor Hazel McCallion supports this observation of crystallized intelligence carrying into advanced years. The mayor of Mississauga, Ontario, Canada, is the longest-serving mayor in Canadian history. Mayor Hazel took office in 1978 when the city had a population of 276,043. Now in her 90s, she actively runs the city and contributes to the well-being of her constituents. The city has doubled its population in the last two decades and is expected to reach 812,000 by the year 2031.

Experiential Intelligence

Experiential intelligence encompasses insight and creativity. It is associated with one's ability to create, invent, discover, and imagine. Experiential intelligence is built upon accumulated knowledge and experience in different areas, covering both formal and informal learning environments over the years. Researchers observed that experiential intelligence can be increased through stimulating learning environments and situations.[28]

A look into history easily demonstrates how individuals can stay creative well into late adulthood. Depending on their areas of work, outstanding creative achievements are seen in artists, scientists, philosophers, and historians. Two examples of outstanding men are cited here, which verifies how both crystallized and experiential intelligence carry into advanced years:

- **Michelangelo Buonarroti:** The Italian renaissance artist and architect demonstrated great talent all his life. His creativity remained strong, if not more prominent, during his second half of life. Michelangelo began painting *The Last Judgment* in the Sistine Chapel at the age of 61, completing it five years later. When he was 71, Michelangelo was appointed as the chief architect of St. Peter's and Farnese Palace.

Visit the website The Age of Happiness: www.ageofhappiness.com to read about today's heroes all around the world who enjoy life and do amazing things at the age of 60, 70, 80, 90 and even into 100.

- **Benjamin Franklin:** One of the seven key founding fathers of the United States of America, Franklin worked tirelessly to fulfill his roles as a prolific writer, inventor, and leader. He helped draft the Declaration of Independence when he was 70 years old; he invented the bifocal lens by age 78. Well into his old age, Franklin continued to read and study. In order to reach high bookshelves, he invented the long arm at the age of 80. The following year, he signed the United States Constituion.

The brilliances of Michelangelo Buonarroti, Benjamin Franklin, and Hazel McCallion are truly inspiring. Their stories demonstrate the power of the human brain and our tenacity. Great things are yet to happen for those who believe and persevere.

But those who hope in the LORD will renew their strength. They will soar on wings like eagles; they will run and not grow weary, they will walk and not be faint.
–Isaiah 40:31

Emotional Intelligence

What is an emotion? It's a natural state of mind, a feeling, a response from circumstances, mood, or relationships with others. An emotion is an impulse to act. For instance, we may cry when we're sad. As human beings, we experience different emotions: joy, serenity, bliss, peace, love, sadness, frustration, hate, horror, fear, anger, anguish, sorrow, the list goes on.

Emotional intelligence (EQ) refers to the ability to perceive, control, evaluate, and manage emotions, which helps you get along with other people. Daniel Goleman, author of the book *Emotional Intelligence*, proposes that personal skills, including self-awareness and empathy, influence one's success in life more so than IQ. Based on his years long reporting on emotions and the brain, Goleman argues that no matter the age, we can learn how to strengthen our relationships with others—and within ourselves.[29] When we pair our emotional and rational minds together, our emotional and intellectual ability improves. By strengthening these domains, we can continue to build friendships by being empathetic, graceful, and poised no matter how old we are.

My late father-in-law was a man of high EQ. He was generous, pleasant, considerate, and dignified. He did not talk much, though when he tried to make a point, everyone would listen carefully. He made friends everywhere he went. Many stories described how he became a successful merchant with a humble beginning, which credited his ability to earn trust from business associates. In his old age, he was still charming and well-liked. The family used to visit a community swimming pool, where the entrance fee was two dollars. But my father-in-law was the exception to this admission because he became friends with the gatekeepers. He gently smiled, waved his right hand and proudly walked through the gates.

Taking Your Intelligence to the Next Level

Today's baby boomers are the "best educated, most literate, and largest generation in history," states Lillian B. Rubin, PhD, author of *60 on Up: The Truth About Aging in America.* So it's understandable why the baby boomer's lifespan is such a hot topic![30]

As you can see, our intelligence level is still in good standing as we age. Blessed with the prospect of a few fruitful decades ahead, our years of insight, experience, hard work, training, successes, and even failures weave into a rich reservoir of crystallized and experiential intelligence. Harnessing the power of our ageless emotional ability, we can continue to enjoy meaningful relationships and impact lives.

Baby boomers are groundbreakers. The idea of lounging in a rocking chair for the next 30 years is probably not what you have in mind. Nor is it likely the aim of younger adults looking ahead to the better half of their lives. We are going to climb new heights to take full advantage of our long lifespan. This book will help turn your ideas into actions and realize your full potential.

Debunking Myth #2: Nature dictates how well we age

According to Dr. Andrew Weil, aging gracefully means, "to let nature take its course while doing everything in our power to delay the onset of aging-related disease." In his book, *Healthy Aging*, Weil states that the prerequisite to aging gracefully is to accept this element: We are getting older every day, so we should not resist this element. We must be realistic about the aging process and understand what happens as we age.[31] The genes from our parents and grandparents are passed on to us, which we have no control over. But, as mentioned earlier, researchers have concluded that the lifestyle choices we make today can determine our health and vitality. Heredity does not have the final say.

When many people think of lifestyle choices, slim tummies, diet plans, nutritional supplements, treadmills, and vacationing on sandy beaches come to mind. However, to me, aging gracefully means to live well in body, mind, and spirit for as long as possible, until we come to our eternal destiny. Since not all literature on aging addresses the spiritual aspect, let us explore the body-mind-spirit connection; these three dimensions are intertwined and well-connected.

Body-Mind-Spirit Connection

The connection between the mind and body has subsisted since the 5th century B.C. Greek physicians alleged that whatever happened in the mind influenced the body, and whatever happened in the body influenced our thought.

Prior to the Greeks, though, the ancient Chinese have always viewed the body, mind, and spirit as integral segments of human beings. Chinese philosophy says that humans and nature are inseparable. What happens in nature affects humans and what man does will directly affect nature. There were periods when the Western medical profession attended to the body for medical diagnosis and treatment, leaving the mind and spirit matters to psychologists, priests, and philosophers. Yet it is becoming more common for modern medical researchers and professionals to consider a mind-body interaction.

What exactly does a person's spirit have to do with his or her physical health? Two modern-day physicians, Dr. Sim I. McMillen and Dr. David E. Stern, wrote *None of These Diseases,* which is based on the Bible's health secrets for the 21st century.[32] McMillen and Stern agree that there is a strong mind-body connection to physical ailments such as diabetes, heart attacks, and arthritis. "A mind upset makes a body sick," write the two doctors. They also suggest there's a link between our mind, body, and spirit. Our spirituality is the linkage between human and God. According to McMillen and Stern, the Bible describes how human beings are created in the "image of God."

To break this idea down, here is an illustration of the mind-body-spirit cycle: the human soul (or spirit) is born with a need to know and experience God. Without an intimate connection with its Creator, the spirit is in turmoil and it longs for ultimate peace, as though a void needs to be filled.

A person may not feel the effect of this void until a trigger goes off. External stress factors, like a job loss, may disrupt the perceived inner peace, making a person aware of his spiritual disharmony. Receiving the signal of internal turmoil, emotions such as fear, anger, or worry kick in. Via the nerves, the brain alerts the physical body with warning bells: the biological glands release adrenaline, cortisone, insulin, and other stress hormones as a response. Then your organs become excessively active—the muscles may spasm, your heartbeat may increase and so forth. Over time, medical conditions such as hypertension, stomachaches, or muscle pain may occur from stress.

My soul yearns for you in the night;
in the morning my spirit longs for you.
–Isaiah 26:9

Multiple Dimensions

Aging gracefully requires us to maintain a balance in all dimensions. In *Unlocking the Mystery of Depression*, author Dr. Clarence Duff analyzes the different aspects of a person. Many distinguishing attributes form the very essence of who and what we are. Duff suggests human beings have psychological, biological, physical, emotional, intellectual, moral, social, and spiritual characteristics that are unlike other forms of animals on earth.[33] Human beings are operating under the influence of all these components, which is why the interplay of these dimensions within a person is complex and fascinating. As an example, when a person suffers a psychological symptom such as depression, it is not enough to trace the problem solely from a psychological dimension. This person may have suffered a prolonged illness that initiated pain, fear, and isolation. The long-term strain of her illness takes a toll on her emotions, causing her to lose hope in life. As a result, it sets off psychological turmoil that manifests as clinical depression.

Equipped with knowledge about the body-mind-spirit connection and our multiple dimensions, the key to aging gracefully is to address the whole person. For now, let's review another commonly believed myth about aging.

Debunking Myth #3: It's too late to change

My close friend is an avid tennis player and loves going to the gym. She plays tennis in the summer and indoor badminton during the winter months. This has been part of her regime since youth till now, at the age of 52. For the longest time, I resented the gym. 20 minutes on an exercise machine seemed like forever. I usually spent the whole time thinking about how much reading or writing I could accomplish, as I grudgingly stepped back and forth on the elliptical. Even worse, I convinced myself it was too late for me to start exercising, since I had never been active. I've already missed out on the benefits of an active lifestyle, so why bother?

I was wrong in believing a myth. Several studies have supported the fact that older individuals (i.e. people in their 60s or 70s) can take measures to preserve and improve their overall health, even if previous lifestyle practices were not optimal. Also, many chronic diseases are preventable with proper nutrition and exercising.

In short, scientific evidence shows that there is much we can do to maintain quality of life, even when changes are initiated at a later age. It's never too late to learn new skills and make lifestyle choices that promote health and vitality. Let's visit the strategies that are instrumental as we strive for longer, healthier, purposeful, and fulfilling lives.

Practical Strategies to Age Gracefully

Aging gracefully involves the well-being of the whole person. Your goal is to stay physically strong, mentally sound, emotionally stable, and spiritually grounded. By spiritually grounded, I mean the general sense of peace in our souls that conveys meaning to our existence. The strategies introduced here are what we can do to promote holistic health, thereby helping us realize our potential now and throughout our retirement years.

Aging gracefully involves the well-being of the whole person. Your goal is to stay physically strong, mentally sound, emotionally stable, and spiritually grounded.

Nourish Your Body

When I visit my doctor for an annual physical checkup, Dr. Ellen always asks how much I exercise per week and whether I have a good appetite. This year she reminded me that I should do at least 120 to 150 minutes of moderate-to-intense physical activity per week. If I enjoy walking, I need to walk three to four times a week. As for my eating habits … well, I need to cut down on my Almond Roca treats. Nevertheless, the key to a strong body is to keep active and eat healthy. Here are a few tips to get you started:

- **Stay active**

A few years ago, when I was struggling with menopause, I was anemic, feeble, and melancholy. Exercising was the last thing on my mind and I told my doctor how I felt. In her professional and caring demeanor, Dr. Ellen explained the importance of physical activities, even in my situation. "Exercise has both a long-term and short-term effect to aging," she explained.

My doctor's advice is consistent with many studies on the benefits of exercise. Exercise can do much more than shed a few pounds. According to Public Health Agency of Canada, physical activity can prevent chronic diseases like cancer, Type 2 diabetes, and heart disease; help boost energy levels and release stress; and prolong good health and independence as we age.[34]

Since everyone has different experiences and preferences in fitness, it's important to consult your doctor and seek the advice of a personal trainer before you start a new exercise routine.

- **Eat healthy**

This may sound clichéd, but it's true: having a well-balanced diet is one of the secrets to good health. I consulted Amanda Li, a Registered Dietitian in Canada, as she shares the five golden rules of healthy eating:

1. ***Eat slowly:*** "It takes 20 minutes for our brains to register that we are full," says Li, who goes on to explain, "If you eat fast, by the time the 'full' signal travels to the brain, you are already over-stuffed."
2. ***Eat only until you are 80 percent full:*** Remember the last time you went to an all-you-can-eat buffet? I bet you felt unpleasantly stuffed! So, "if you eat until you are almost full, you no longer feel hungry and you will not pack on the extra calories," says Li.
3. ***Eat foods that represent all the colors of the rainbow:*** According to Li, nature has packed beneficial, healthy compounds into bright-colored fruits and vegetables. For instance, blueberries help to keep the mind sharp, whereas ruby-hued tomatoes may contribute to preventing prostate

cancer. "Eating from all the colors of the rainbow will ensure that you obtain all the nutrients, vitamins, minerals, and phytochemicals (anti-oxidants) that you need," assures Li.

4. ***Eat mostly plant foods and everything else in moderation:*** "Animal products are a good source of protein and iron. However, they are high in saturated fats," says Li. Unfortunately, a diet high in saturated fats is a major risk factor for cardiovascular disease. Therefore, Li says, "plant foods such as lentils, chickpeas, nuts, and seeds are rich in protein and iron that our bodies can absorb."
5. ***Limit processed foods*** (i.e. any foods that can last more than two weeks without preservation): Boxed foods (macaroni and cheese, chicken nuggets, TV dinners, frozen pizzas, hot dogs, instant noodles, cookies, potato chips) are usually high in calories and have little nutritional value. Plus, they contain refined flour, additional sugar, and sodium and they are high in fat. Not to mention, many of these boxed foods have preservatives and artificial coloring. Li recommends minimizing these types of foods and when you do, "you are more likely eating fruits, vegetables, and whole grains such as brown rice, quinoa, or buckwheat."

It's never too late to start exercising and to adopt these healthy eating habits. Studies by Dr. Richard S. Rivlin—as published in the *American Journal of Clinical Nutrition*—have shown that people in their 60s and older can still benefit greatly from positive eating habits.[35] However, Rivlin makes a sound point: it's important to seek professional help in devising a plan. Your plan must be suitable for your build, dietary restrictions, physical condition, and preferences, as Rivlin believes there's no such thing as a "one-size-fits-all" diet.

Nourish Your Mind

A heart at peace gives life to the body, but envy rots the bones.
–Proverbs 14:30

A cheerful heart is good medicine, but a crushed spirit dries up the bones.
– Proverbs 17:22

Just like the body, our minds need stimulation to stay sharp. Neurologists are finding that our brains have the ability to generate new brain cells. This is true even into old age, though at a slower rate than when we were younger. Though we can't stop the clock, nor predict if we'll develop age-related dementia, we have some control over the rate of brain decline. You can maintain good mental and emotional health by:

- **Seeking peace of mind:** Dr. Don Colbert's book, *Deadly Emotions,* discusses how depression, anger, guilt, condemnation, and low self-esteem are toxic emotions that threaten body and spirit health. Colbert challenges his readers to apply biblical principles by focusing on the power of forgiveness and repentance, a joyful heart, and a divine connection with our Heavenly Father.[36] We can't control another person or unpleasant circumstances. However, we can choose to free our mind from dwelling on problems, past hurt, and negative thoughts.

- **Remaining engaged with social connectedness:** Try to expand your heart and mind by serving someone in need. Or extend a hug or smile to someone discouraged. Sharing fun times with your loved ones or contributing to someone's happiness brings delight and enriches our own lives.

- **Engaging in continuous learning:** I believe in being older and growing rather than simply saying I'm growing old. The day I choose to stop learning is the day I choose to stop growing. Keep your curiosity aroused—explore things outside your comfort zone. Try reading a book on an unusual subject or walking a new trail you've never strolled along before. If you don't do it this year, you'll be a year older when you do. Develop interests, learn a new skill, or upgrade some existing skills by taking a class or through self-study. We can all experience satisfaction from doing something enjoyable. It is the best therapy for relaxing the mind.

Nourish Your Spirit

"...death is the birthing passage to a new life."
–Joan Chittister, author of *The Gift of Years: Growing Older Gracefully*

We established earlier how the human spirit is born with a need to know and experience God. He speaks about this fact eloquently through the psalmist:

He has made everything beautiful in its time.
He has also set eternity in the human heart...
–Ecclesiastes 3:11

Although our body will wear out and our mind may gradually regress, our spirit will never grow old. Each day puts us one day closer to our eternal destiny. God's desire is for us to know Him more intimately. He is awaiting our return to Him with open arms. Nurturing our spirit is about sharpening the awareness of

Although our body will wear out and our mind may gradually regress, our spirit will never grow old. Each day puts us one day closer to our eternal destiny.

God's presence in our lives. Our Heavenly Father longs to abide in us when we give Him attention. That said, I recommend these steps: slow down, read His word, pray, do what is right, and live your life purpose.

- **Slow down**
  - If you're like most people in North America, you're living a hectic schedule. Even during retirement, retirees may have appointments, gatherings, trips to the mall, and chores that occupy their waking hours. Spending quiet time to connect with God, our Maker, is a very unnatural activity. Spiritual leaders encourage us to practice solitude often. God reminds us in Psalms 46:10, to: *"Be still, and know that I am God."*

Henri Nouwen, author of *Making All Things New: An Invitation to the Spiritual Life,* describes our hurried life: "Our occupations and preoccupations fill our external and internal lives to the brim. They prevent the Spirit of God from breathing freely in us and thus renewing our lives."[37] Our busyness often leaves us feeling filled yet unfulfilled. Devote some time each day to focus on God and have fellowship with him.

- **Read the Bible**
  - We know God by reading the Bible. *"In the beginning was the Word, and the Word was with God, and the Word was God"* (John 1:1). The more time one spends with the Word, the more the Word will come alive.

Some people refer to the Bible as the love letter from God to human. This is something you have to try and taste. If you're new to the Bible, start with the Gospel of John. Then read the rest of the Gospel books, followed by the Psalms and Proverbs. By then, you will likely be drawn to reading more.

When you use a systematic method of studying this precious book, your worldview will change. People who regularly study the

Bible meditate on His words and pray. Many testify how the Bible's truth never grows stale. The more they read, the more profound insight they are able to glean. This is also my experience. (If you don't own a Bible, you can read the Bible online for free by visiting www.biblegateway.com.

- **Pray**
  - If slowing down feels unnatural, praying may feel like that, too. We have to consciously put our wandering mind and racing heart on hold, to focus on God while we pray. Prayer is two-way communication. Through prayer, we offer our praise, our confession, our thanksgiving and supplications to God. God, in turn, responds to us through inspiration, convictions, and circumstances. I encourage you to write down your special prayers and review them from time to time. Be amazed at how God answers your prayers in His timing and style.

- **Do what is right**

And let us not lose heart and grow weary and faint in acting nobly and doing right, for in due time and at the appointed season we shall reap, if we do not loosen and relax our courage and faint.
–Galatians 6:9, AMP

- Practice what you learn from the Bible. Do what's right for you with perseverance and discipline. Aging gracefully requires intention, commitment, and effort. We still have lots of potential to grow. Expect to work hard and give all you've got in sustaining growth.

Whatever you do, work at it with all your heart, as working for the Lord…
–Colossians 3:23

- **Live your life purpose**

Forgetting what is behind and straining toward what is ahead, I press on toward the goal to win the prize for which God has called me heavenward in Christ Jesus.
–Philippians 4:13–14

  - Discovering God's plan for your life is the most rewarding experience. Imagine finishing life without knowing why you were put on this earth. It's time to find that purpose. Remember, focus on the end result, grow your potential, and live it out daily. Finally, claim that prize when you arrive at your eternal home.

Long life is a symbol of blessing for many cultures. The Bible also regards long life as blessings from the Almighty. When Solomon was installed as king at a young age, God promised to lengthen his days if he obeyed and followed His instructions, as his father David did.

McMillen and Stern, the authors of *None of these Diseases*, advocate how the Bible contains valuable prescriptions for living a healthy lifestyle. They summarize research findings that point to weekly church attendance, daily Bible reading, and a constant attitude of prayer as the prescription for healthy living—in all three dimensions of body, mind, and spirit. Their conclusion is: "Faith makes fit, and doubt makes sick."[38]

The above strategies can be adopted to preserve stamina in our body, mind, and spirit, and to help lower the risk of diseases. However, we're growing older each day and we all face some levels of unwelcomed, age-related decline. We can't change the inevitable. Pastor, author, and Bible teacher Chuck Swindoll teaches us the importance of embracing the right attitudes each day. On my bedroom wall, a poster with his famous quote says, "Life is 10% what happens to me and 90% how I react to it. And so it is with you… we are in charge of our attitudes."

Let's explore three attitudes that significantly impact our ability to age gracefully.

Three Winning Attitudes to Age Gracefully

Research findings have demonstrated the links between a positive outlook in life and good health. Knowing the facts, opportunities, and limitations associated with getting older can help us advance into the next leg of our journey with optimism. According to a study of 660 men and women aged 50 and older from Ohio, conducted by Becca Levy from Yale University, people with positive identities on aging lived 7.6 years longer than those with negative perceptions.[39]

So what does it take to cultivate positive self-perception? Here are the three winning attitudes:

1. Adopt a growing mindset

Everything is possible for one who believes.
–Mark 9:23

According to her book, *Mindset: The New Psychology of Success*, Dr. Carol S. Dweck deems that everyone has one of two basic mindsets: fixed or growth.[40] Those with fixed mindsets believe their talents and abilities are set in stone; they either have it or they don't. The sad news is that those with fixed mindsets remain on a motionless path. On the other hand, people with growth mindsets are aware that talents can be developed and how those great abilities are built over time; this mindset leads to the path of opportunity and success.

2. Think positive

Whatever is true, whatever is noble, whatever is right, whatever is pure, whatever is lovely, whatever is admirable—if anything is excellent or praiseworthy—think about such things.
–Philippians 4:8

There are different perspectives to viewing people, objects, or situations. Seeing a glass as half full or half empty are two different means of describing the same thing. Do you tend to see the bright side or do you dwell on the negative? Feeding your mind with positive thoughts is the starting point to steering yourself towards optimism, a positive attitude, and resilience in the face of hardship.

3. Commit to lifelong learning

Do not conform to the pattern of this world,
but be transformed by the renewing of your mind.
–Romans 12:2

Continuous learning promotes personal growth, which introduces new ways of thinking. This equips a person with new skills and ideas. It also enables a person to achieve his or her potential in life. As you learn new things, be ready to change old habits and allow fresh knowledge to shape new behaviors.

I invite you to reflect on the following questions. Respond to each one with an open mind. Your responses will form an action plan, which you can follow as you commit to strategies for aging gracefully in body, mind, and spirit.

REVIEW QUESTIONS

1. My Physical Activity

a. Which physical activities do I enjoy most?

b. When can I start doing one of the above activities regularly?

c. What do I need to do to perform that activity regularly?

d. Which physical activities do I currently do and need to continue?

e. What unhealthy habits do I need to stop doing?

f. Are there any obstacles preventing me from stopping that unhealthy habit?

g. What do I need to do to stop that habit?

2. My Emotional Well-Being

a. What are my current methods for relaxing or de-stressing?

b. Are there any other ways I can de-stress or relax? If yes, what are they?

c. What do I need to do to start that new relaxing activity on a regular basis?

d. Do I have built-up toxic emotions in me (e.g. anger, bitterness, guilt, etc.)?

e. What are the obstacles that hinder me to:
   i. Relieve my anger towards…?
   ii. Let go of the hurt, condemnation, bitterness, guilt of…?
   iii. Forgive the people who have done wrong to me?
   iv. Forgive myself for the things I did not appreciate doing?

f. What do I need to do to restore my peace of mind?

3. My Spiritual Well-Being

a. Which activities do I enjoy the most that also bring me closer to God?

b. If I haven't yet, when can I start doing one of the above activities on a regular basis?

c. What do I need to do to start doing that activity regularly?

d. Which habits do I have that cause me to stumble in my faith?

e. Are there any obstacles that need to be removed for me to change this negative habit?

f. What do I need in order to stop that negative habit?

g. Which habits or behaviors do I need to continue?

SUMMARY

In this chapter, we debunked three myths contrary to the physical and mental dexterity of the middle aged. We reviewed the highlights of various forms of intelligence. We discussed how you can maximize the tremendous resource of your brain, expanding on your crystallized, experiential, and emotional intelligence. With this chapter's practical strategies for aging gracefully in body, mind, and spirit, along with embracing winning attitudes, you are set for lifelong service and longevity.

four

WHY PLANNING WORKS FOR THE LONG HAUL

"All of God's people are ordinary people who have been made extraordinary by the purpose He has given them."
–Oswald Chambers, author of *My Utmost for His Highest*

"Trust in the LORD with all your heart and lean not on your own understanding; in all your ways submit to him, and he will make your paths straight."
Proverbs 3:5–6

"Failing to plan is planning to fail."
–Benjamin Franklin (1706–1790), scientist, inventor

"Planning is bringing the future into the present so that you can do something about it now."
–Alan Lakein, author, time management guru

WITH THE ADVANCEMENT OF MEDICINE AND TECHNOLOGY, WE'RE enjoying better health than our forefathers. Consequently, we may be living much longer than we originally expected! According to

Statistics Canada, in 2008 men were reportedly spending 15 years in retirement; for women, their retirement endured for about 19 years.[41] So what can you achieve in the next 10, 20, or 30 years?

Planning allows you to break down your goals and strategically approach each year of your retirement with purpose and intention. Here, I would like you to meet Cindy, a baby boomer who demonstrates how planning and perseverance are advantageous to any retirement.

Baby Boomer Role Model: Cindy

Cindy was dressed in her white lab coat, treating her last patient of the day at a school clinic. But this wasn't just any ordinary day for Cindy; it was the final day of her four long years of intensive study at the Toronto School of Traditional Chinese Medicine (TSTCM).

Well into her late 50s, Cindy opened her private practice as a Chinese medicine practitioner and acupuncturist. Truly, the retirement years had served a new chapter in Cindy's life. Being a Traditional Chinese Medicine (TCM) practitioner is Cindy's second career. She previously worked full-time as a senior manager for a bank and retired early to pursue other interests. However, during her first few years of retirement, she didn't have anything particular to focus on (although she was active in her church community). One day her son, Aric, who had recently graduated from his bachelor degree program, mentioned his desire to enroll at TSTCM. Cindy was curious about the opportunity and asked Aric if she could tag along with him to his school orientation. Soon after, both Cindy and Aric started their journey in TCM studies.

It took Cindy a little over four years to complete the vigorous advanced TCM diploma program, which consisted of 4,220 semester hours in lectures, a clinical internship, and research studies. Though Cindy was unintentionally introduced to TCM, she knew this was the field for her after the first few courses. Her desire to use this knowledge to help her family and friends grew stronger and with vitality. It became her end goal, which encouraged Cindy to be diligent in her studies toward launching this new career.

Throughout Cindy's studies, she would map out her priorities, especially at the beginning of each semester. She also asked her family for help with house chores so she could bury herself in books and research. Now, Cindy is thrilled to use her newfound skills in promoting healthy living and treating patients. As a role model, she truly encourages others to be bold and follow their dreams—ones they've always wanted to explore or those discovered later in life.

Blueprint for Your Future

Do you have moments when time seems to slip away in the blink of an eye? My friend's college-aged daughter, for example, never made up her mind as to what she wanted to do during the summertime. One day, my friend said in frustration that his daughter would sit by the window all morning, staring at the neighbor's kids on the street. She said she was busy planning her day. But the afternoon would come and then the evening would roll in. She claimed she was still contemplating her plans. Days or weeks would pass before she took any serious action. By the time she figured it out, summer was over and school started again.

You can probably identify with my friend's frustration and agree that his daughter should have planned. When it comes to your retirement, a thought-out plan serves as a blueprint for your future. Though depending on your personality, planning may not be your favorite activity. You may even be turned off by planning because you've never followed through with plans before! Maybe you don't like being tied down to a schedule, or maybe you would rather be spontaneous, engaging in certain activities at the spur of the moment. However, life experiences may

> Having a plan enables you to be in control of what you want to achieve.

tell us that last-minute deals don't always exist. And even if they do exist, you may have to pay a premium to get what you want; otherwise, you may miss out altogether.

Having a plan enables you to be in control of what you want to achieve. You can take ownership of the future outcome because you're not leaving it up to chance. (The later chapters will guide you through the planning process step by step.) Here are more reasons planning works for your retirement:

- ***Things Don't Happen 'Just Because'***

Any worthwhile cause requires planning. Great opportunities rarely fall in your lap; you have to make an effort for them to happen. The examples from Cindy's journey and my friend's daughter illustrate this principle. Akin to traveling plans, you need to book your flight, car, and accommodations ahead of time. Stand-by and walk-in deals may not exist and even if they do, they will take more time and money in the end.

- ***Planning Gives You Flexibility***

It may sound counter-intuitive to say that planning gives us flexibility—though it does make life much easier. Once, my former mentor revealed that his secret to success was his calendar. At the beginning of each year, he would review all the past year's significant events and recurring activities. Then he worked on his New Year calendar by marking down the recurring activities that he needed to continue, plus new appointments and traveling plans. As a committed Christian and family man, he also booked days for dinners and church retreats. Since he had this calendar set out early in the year, he could easily juggle his schedule as unplanned events arose. The calendar kept him organized despite his hectic schedule, giving him a sense of control. Plus, my former mentor could easily see windows of opportunities to fit in new sales calls or spontaneous activities.

- ***Planning Propels You to Accomplish a Goal***

Just like education and career planning, retirement planning serves the same purpose, allowing us to meet our retirement goals. However, retirement planning connects us to the finish line, helping us take the necessary steps in achieving a life mission. We do not know how much more time we have for this mission—we only know that we've already used up 40, 50, or 60 years to date. We want to maximize our remaining years and succeed in this goal before our time is up.

Let me paint you a less favorable picture: If you know your calling, but you have never taken the time to consider how to achieve it in a holistic scheme, you will likely fumble in making progress. On the contrary, if you have a vague idea of what you want to do and know your next few steps, you might achieve some targets without actualizing your final goal; this is because the road to the destination seems remote, distant, and broad. So, let's say you want to write a book: you know you'll have to upgrade your skills first. You may go as far as signing up for a writing course or even completing the class. But wait a minute—what about crafting a book proposal and working on the rest of the steps needed for completing your project? Without a solid plan, you'll likely miss the mark in utilizing your talents, skills, and experience to accomplish that end goal.

- ***Planning Makes You Accountable***

A plan with detailed steps drives accountability for one's actions. If you have a plan in place and a step is missed, you become aware of it immediately and take action for continuing progress. This keeps you moving forward. Also, the thought process that has gone into the plan generates a sense of ownership over the goal; you've made a conscious decision to carry out the tasks for meeting the end target.

- ***Planning Gives You a Reality Check***

Life is unpredictable, which is where retirement planning kicks in. A plan can be revised or tasks can be postponed, yet you can continue moving in the right direction. In other words, prescribed steps in a plan keep track of our progress, allowing us to start, pause, or resume. A plan enables us to deal with the following realities of being human:

a) Interruptions
Last November, I set aside a chunk of time to write this book. An early morning phone call caused me to put this agenda item on hold until further notice: I needed to look after my mom, as she was hit by a car during her usual morning walk. Thankfully, she suffered a non-fatal head injury and recovered at a gradual pace. Four weeks later, my mom was able to care for herself and I resumed the task that was left off. In my plan, I had set out milestones to guide my writing progress. My next milestone at the time was to complete two chapters by the end of December. A four-week schedule delay naturally translated into a four-week extension in my next milestone. But I decided to put in extra time to compensate, without missing the milestone dates. Having a detailed plan with milestones and tangible outcomes kept me on target.

b) Distractions
Do you recall adjusting your schedule for unexpected events? Maybe friends were in town for a surprise visit, and somehow you adjusted your schedule to accommodate their stay. You temporarily detoured from your planned activities but you got back on track after they left. On the other hand, if you're busy pursuing your planned activities, saying no to engagements that don't align with your goals may be necessary. Avoiding distraction from your grand scheme is a valid option.

c) Distress
When a loved one passes away, we need time to grieve. When we're faced with critical illness, we have to take a break from our activities to deal with our predicament. If God provides us with more years on earth, we need to be obedient and live out His

purpose with the time we have left. We resume our plans when the circumstances allow. A plan is a map to fulfilling our life purpose one day at a time.

- ***Planning Enables Support***

Your plan can work as a tool for communicating with others about your goals and how they can help you achieve them. In general, people are eager to offer help if they're aware of your specific needs, especially when help is requested explicitly. This reminds me of the moral from my favorite fable, *The Alchemist.* Author Paolo Coelho encourages us to follow our dreams and live out our personal legend because "[w]hen you want something, all the universe conspires in helping you to achieve it." You will be pleasantly surprised to learn how many people want to help you attain your life purpose. Share your best-laid plans with others, rally support, and see yourself living your best.

- ***Planning Spurs Excitement***

A plan gives us hope that we can achieve an outcome. As you make progress and check off your completed steps, the destination becomes closer at hand. You feel excited by looking at how far you've progressed, realizing how success is only within reach. A solid plan propels you to move forward with positive energy.

What Makes a Sound Plan?

As a professional project manager for more than 15 years, I've come across a handful of successful projects where goals were met on time and within budget. Though I've seen projects that never met the dawn of day, projects cancelled due to budget constraints or because they failed to deliver the desired results. Not to mention, it's very common to see finished projects that meet only partial goals after exceeding the initial budget and timeline.

As explained in *Alpha Project Managers: What the Top 2% Know That Everyone Else Does Not,* author Andy Crowe surveyed more than 860 international project managers to highlight which traits make them stand out as superior or, in other words, alpha according to their teams, executives, and customers. One of the interesting findings from the book is that 'alpha project managers' spent twice as much time in the planning phase of their projects than non-alphas.[42] Hence, planning is critical for project success.

A thorough plan has the following characteristics that can be applied to retirement planning:

- A sound plan begins with a clear purpose.
  - What makes you unique?
  - What are you called to do that allows you to fully live out your special purpose on earth?

- A sound plan has a well-defined scope.
  - Which activities do you enjoy the most?
  - What result or outcome would you deliver?

- A sound plan is doable.
  - Is what you have in mind achievable within your capacity and ability?
  - Will you be able to follow through with your plan?

- A sound plan includes risk assessment.
  - What are the risk factors that may negatively impact your goals?
  - What are some appropriate strategies that may help mitigate each risk?

- A sound plan makes room for progressive elaboration. (As you execute your plan, you'll likely discover more facts, opportunities, or constraints that require you to elaborate your detailed steps.)
  - How can you improve your plan to make a greater impact?
  - Is there room for more improvement?

The second-last chapter of this book is devoted to the nuts and bolts of planning your work and working your plan. And don't worry, I'm here for you—I have tools ready for you to develop a measurable action plan. This will help you focus your energy on aspects that are aligned with your calling.

Summary

We are certainly living longer than our forefathers and enjoying better health. Our outlook for the future is promising. No matter what stage your life journey is at, you may still have many bountiful years to live. We need a sound plan to guide us to a purposeful and fulfilling journey ahead. As this chapter presents the characteristics of a sound plan and what makes it valuable, you are well-equipped to start planning. Get ready to proceed to Part III of this book. There, you will begin a journey of discovering who you are and how you can live out God's plan.

"May he give you the desire of your heart
and make all your plans succeed."
–Psalm 20:4

Part Three

DISCOVERING YOURSELF

Discover who you are and celebrate your personality, life gifts, passion, and value. You are the only one in this world who can accomplish God's plan for your life. Be inspired to live out this special calling.

five

WHAT DOES THE BIBLE SAY ABOUT HIS PLAN FOR YOUR LIFE?

"'For I know the plans I have for you,' declares the LORD,
'plans to prosper you and not to harm you,
plans to give you hope and a future.'"
–Jeremiah 29:11

"Not everything that counts can be counted,
and not everything that can be counted counts."
–Albert Einstein (1879–1955), physicist, Nobel Prize recipient

"I will instruct you and teach you in the way you should go;
I will counsel you with my loving eye on you."
–Psalm 32:8

MY CHURCH FRIEND RECENTLY WENT THROUGH HARD TIMES, AND grew stronger in faith despite her trials. She later commented that the Bible has all the answers for her day-to-day living. Similarly, my pastor just started a new preaching series titled, *When in doubt, consult the instruction manual [the Bible]*. In Chapters 1 and 2, we've explored the biblical concept of lifelong service. Here, let's review two biblical principles regarding God's plan for our lives, namely: priorities and choices.

PRIORITIES AND CHOICES

In the Old Testament, God spoke directly to the new leader of Israel, Joshua, after Moses' death. God instructed Joshua to cling to the book of the law day and night. This included reading it, speaking about it, and acting upon all that is written. God promised that Joshua would enjoy prosperity and success (Joshua 1:8). And he did. Joshua chose to remain strong and courageous as he took up the leadership role. He was determined in following God's instructions.

In the New Testament, Jesus sums up the Ten Commandments into two (Matthew 22:37–39): First, *"Love the Lord your God with all your heart and with all your soul and with all your mind."* Second, *"Love your neighbor as yourself."* God desires a loving relationship with us and He expects us to love one another.

Throughout the Bible, we learn about the blessings of God and our responsibilities to live righteous lives following kingdom principles. Can we derive our priorities and choices in life based on the above principles and directives? In our modern society, it's challenging to live out our Christian beliefs and values. Walking by sight is more popular than walking by faith. But the challenge was the same even in Joshua's time, or in the New Testament era. Choosing to heed God's instructions is not the mainstream. Yet, God is faithful. He has plans to prosper us and give us a hopeful future, including our retirement years.

Walking by sight is more popular than walking by faith.

MISPLACED PRIORITIES ALERT

In today's culture, women are investing in methods to turn back the clock: diet pills, personal training, makeup and anti-wrinkle concoctions, mud baths, invasive and non-invasive cosmetic surgery, you name it. Even men are getting in on this game, though to a lesser degree.

Why are people electing to spend their hard-earned money and precious time, and to withstand the possibility of adverse side effects to hold on to their youthful look for as long as they can? Turning back the clock is about maintaining the status quo. We are comfortable with our younger appearance and perhaps apprehensive about ourselves as we actually are at present and might be forthcoming. Perhaps focusing on anti-wrinkle treatments or tummy tucks is easier to deal with rather than embracing the reality of advancing to a new phase of life. Perhaps delaying the inevitable stems from our fear about the future.

Fear is opposite to faith. Fear can paralyze our judgment and cause us to misplace our priorities on secondary matters rather than what's primary. In the example of Joshua, instead of fear, he exhibited ruthless faith. Joshua remained strong and courageous to counter the unknown as he stepped up to his leadership role.

Fear can paralyze our judgment and cause us to misplace our priorities on secondary matters rather than what's primary.

Discovering and accepting God's plan in our lives requires us to remain faithful and take risks. In the Old Testament, a woman named Esther used her gifts and unique position to accomplish God's work. Esther could have stuck with being beautiful and subservient, and as time wore on tried her best to maintain that beauty despite its inevitable fading. She showed the courage of taking a huge risk, instead. Esther changed history.

A Beauty Queen Story

The Bible hints at how women maintained their beauty during the ancient days. The Book of Esther describes young ladies preparing for a national beauty contest to win the title of Queen of Persia in 480 B.C. Contestants had to complete 12 months of prescribed beauty treatments, including a six-month treatment with oil of myrrh, followed by six months of perfumes and cosmetics. Esther was naturally gorgeous. Officials provided Esther with expensive cosmetics and they placed her on a special diet upon entering the contest. Her stunning beauty won the admiration of everyone she met.

> *For if you remain silent at this time, relief and deliverance for the Jews will arise from another place, but you and your father's family will perish. And who knows but that you have come to your royal position for such a time as this?*
> –Esther 4:14

Esther was a Jewish orphan raised by her cousin and foster parent, Mordecai, who was exiled from Jerusalem. Being Jewish and living life as an exile was a constant threat in this violent world. The tide turned when Esther won the title of Queen of Persia. However, she was later challenged by another life-and-death ordeal: the King's highest official, Haman, instigated to kill Mordecai and his fellow Jews, as Mordecai refused to bow and pay homage to him. The King somehow agreed to Haman's wicked plot.

Esther had two choices: She could remain silent and maintain her status quo. Or, she could plead for the King to revoke the decree to kill all the Jews in Persia. But the second choice involved risking death, since no one was allowed to approach the King except when summoned by him. Esther took courage and strategically planned her petition. She confronted the King and implored him to withdraw the eradication. Esther recognized the criticality of her daunting task and the limitations she faced. By faith, she called upon all the Jews in Susa to fast with her for three days and nights before confronting the King, a confrontation that was against the law. She left the outcome to God: *"If I perish, I perish"* (Esther 4:16).

God's Plan for You

Just as God equipped Esther to save the Jews from extermination, God also has a plan for your life. Let's turn to four Bible passages that discuss how you already have an important responsibility in His grand kingdom.

- You are created in the image of God. (Genesis 1:26–27)
- You are one and only. (Psalm 139:13–16)
- God has in mind specific good works for you to accomplish. (Ephesians 2:10)
- You are called to be the light and salt of this world. (Matthew 5:13–16)

Created in God's Image

Then God said, "Let us make mankind in our image, in our likeness, so that they may rule over the fish in the sea and the birds in the sky, over the livestock and all the wild animals, and over all the creatures that move along the ground."
So God created mankind in his own image, in the image of God he created them; male and female he created them.
–Genesis 1:26–27

You are created after God's likeness. You are made of Godly substance, with resemblances and some qualities of God that other creatures do not have. The passage above assures that you have the spirituality and characteristics of the divine Creator. God made you to have superior qualities and capabilities to govern other life forms around you.

You Are One and Only

My frame was not hidden from you when I was made in the secret place, when I was woven together in the depths of the earth. Your eyes saw my unformed body; all the days ordained

for me were written in your book before one of them came to be.
–Psalm 139:15–16

A hand-knit sweater, blanket, scarf, or hat is a personal gift unlike any other. Knitting takes time and creativity. You knit or purl one stitch at a time, delicately weaving the piece of yarn between your hands and fingers with a pair of needles. The combination of colors, textures, and designs becomes endless. So when the Bible says, "He knit you together in your mother's womb," this is how God created each of us in a distinctive way.

Made for Good Deeds

For we are God's handiwork, created in Christ Jesus to do good works, which God prepared in advance for us to do.
–Ephesians 2:10

In 2012, the world's population hit the historic seven-billion mark. The fascinating fact is that none of the seven billion people on this earth are identical. Every day in 1997, about 365,000 babies were born.[43] Using the words of the psalmist, imagine how God knits each baby with wonderful love, care, and special design. The Creator arranges each little detail that needs to be in place. Before a baby is born, all the days of his or her life are designed and written into the book of life. He further molds and shapes each person into a piece of art "handiwork" in order to carry out "good works" as told by the above Bible verse. God has in mind specific responsibilities for you to accomplish. You and I are not made from a cookie cutter or random experiment. God prepared you as a special instrument for Him to use.

Light and Salt

You are the salt of the earth. But if the salt loses its saltiness, how can it be made salty again? …
You are the light of the world. A town built on a hill cannot be hidden. Neither do people light a lamp and put it under a bowl. Instead they put it on its stand, and it gives light to everyone in the house. In the same way, let your light shine before others, that they may see your good deeds and glorify your Father in heaven.
–Matthew 5:13–16

What is God's expectation in your special role and good deeds? The answer is in the above passage. So if you were made as salt, your job would be to add taste to food. If you were a lamp, you would provide light.

Think of how you can enrich the people in this world. We are created to be relational beings. You enjoy your blessings and impact other lives. This passage talks about being the light of the world and letting that light shine. This may refer to brightening up someone who feels hopeless, bringing hope to the less fortunate, or shedding light on gloomy and desperate situations. No matter what part God designed for you to play, do it well to exhibit your special function, to glorify your Heavenly Father.

What Makes You Exceptional?

Have you ever spotted two of the same snowflakes? Scientists have observed that no two snowflakes are alike. Just like snowflakes, God created every one of us distinctively. Consider your height, size, complexion, eye color, hair, body shape, and facial features—these visible biological differences make each of us one and only.

Can you think of other characteristics that make you different? Refer to the following list to help you out. This exercise captures what you already know about yourself. As you follow through this list, I invite you to jot down whatever comes to mind. Try to write at least one response for each line. If you can't think of an answer, come back to the question later before moving on to the next section. There is no need for you to over-analyze the question or your response. Allow your intuition to take over.

My Talents

When I was young, people said I was good at _______________.
In the workplace, I get complimented on ___________________.

My Personality

Most of the time, I feel ___________________ about life.
When I am at my finest and best, my friends say I am ________.
I feel stressed when __________________________________.
When I am stressed, I usually ____________________________.
In conflicting situations, I usually ________________________.
I feel most energized when ______________________________.
In my family, I am the (loudest, quickest to act, etc.) ________.
I am most proud of myself when _________________________.
I enjoy a good laugh when ______________________________.

My Interests

In my spare time, I enjoy ______________________________.
To me, leisure means __________________________________.

My Values and Beliefs

I live by these core values in life: ________________________.
What I want most in life is _____________________________.
My belief system includes: _____________________________.

My Culture

I am most proud of my cultural background in these areas:
____.

My Education

My education achievements include: ____________________.
The subject(s) I enjoy most are: ________________________.
If I were to go back to school, I would study ______________.

My Family/Childhood

In my family, I am the (oldest/middle sibling/youngest) .
My favorite childhood activities were: ___________________.
A memorable time during my childhood was _____________.

My Social Circle

My best friends are ______________________________.
I enjoy spending time with ___________________________.

My Profession

My dream job looks like this: ________________________.
These would be my tasks in my dream job: ______________.
(For homemakers only) I am good at____________________.

My Experience

These are the key experiences that have shaped who I am:

____

____

____

____

As you review your responses, you will feel truly amazed. Recognize what makes you different. Your uniqueness affects the way you live, the way you view the world, the way you interact with people. It also shapes your communication, leadership style, conflict resolution skills, and lifestyle choices. Let's celebrate who you are and move on to a fast-paced journey of self-discovery.

Summary

We may not know why two snowflakes are not the same. But we do know that God created us to fulfill His purpose through creation. In this chapter, you have reviewed how God guided and groomed Esther to achieve her deeds, with a great responsibility for the deliverance of the Jews. Knowing that you are noble with holy attributes and that God has a plan for you, ask yourself this question: how do you take this knowledge and apply it to your life? Do you see God's plan unfolding before your eyes? I believe you have an important part to play on earth. In the next few chapters, you'll dive into your life gifts, personality traits, strengths, weaknesses, values, and passion.

six

DEFINING YOUR LIFE GIFTS

"Every good and perfect gift is from above, coming down from the Father of the heavenly lights, who does not change like shifting shadows."
–James 1:17

"Our talents are God's gift to us.
What we make of our talents is our gift back to God."
–Leo Buscaglia (1924–1998), author and motivational speaker

"The soul without imagination is
what an observatory would be without a telescope."
–Henry Ward Beecher, American Minister

When you meet a person for the first time, sometimes you can quickly spot his innate ability. My friend Anthony is a prime example of someone who radiates his life gift: speaking. His gift was evident when he was a young child and, to this day, he can captivate audiences to big cheers or great tears. As he continues to nurture this gift through training and practice, he has further become a polished speaker.

Each individual has his or her own life gifts. Discovering your unique life gifts is the first step in finding your life purpose. In this chapter, you will take an inventory of your life gifts, talents, and special skills.

> Everyone is gifted; but some people never open their package.
> –Anonymous

WHAT ARE LIFE GIFTS?

A life gift describes a person's natural ability in doing something well. Life gifts are a special blend of interests and abilities that make up your unique design. They are something you are born with, that you are inexplicably and innately good at. Some other characteristics of life gifts include:

Life gifts are a special blend of interests and abilities that make up your unique design.

- When you use your gifts, they bring joy to you and the people around you.
- You look forward to using these gifts.
- In extreme cases, you feel like you're in a "zone" when you do them.
- Time seems to fly by when you perform these gifts.
- You don't get tired or sick of these life gifts.
- You have a sense of fulfillment when you make use of them.

The term "life gift" is inspired by the Bible verse found in Proverbs regarding parental instructions: *"Train up a child in the way he should go [and in keeping with his individual gift or bent], and when he is old he will not depart from it"* (Proverbs 22:6, AMP). The authors of *Lifekeys: Discover Who You Are*, David Stark, Jane A. G.

Kise, and Sandra Krebs Hirsh, expounded the meaning of this verse: parents are instructed to teach, guide, direct and educate their child according to the way that fits his needs; even if he becomes old, he will not turn away from it.[44] The key is to allow the child to keep his individual gift or "bent." Bent, as defined by the *New Oxford American Dictionary*, is a "natural talent or inclination."

From observing the growth of my children, I can share examples of their life gifts (which you might be able to relate to):

Ginny: My oldest daughter has the life gift of synthesizing information. When she was young, going to the library was her favorite pastime. She would sift through the juvenile novel section and, within a few minutes, return with a stack of 10 to fifteen books! Two days later, she'd finish the books and ask to visit the library again. I believe, as Ginny matured, her exposure to a variety of genres, plus her analytical bent, contributed to her academic and early career success. She was a popular teacher, a sought-after project analyst, and is now studying to be a litigation lawyer.

Amanda: My second daughter has the life gift of public speaking. In kindergarten, Amanda would practice her show-and-tell time at home. She would rifle through her toy box, choose a Barbie doll or an aluminum toy toaster, then rehearse what she would say to her class. As she grew up, she loved entertaining guests, sharing with everyone her secret dinner recipes and food tips. Now a registered dietitian for a leading food company, Amanda conducts grocery tours and nutritional presentations.

What are Talents?

A talent is a natural ability in doing something well. However, you may not have a passion for it or you may not look forward to doing it all the time. If you have a specific talent, you can pick up the skill relatively easily with a bit of training or guidance; you possess the aptitude for doing it, and you feel competent when you perform it.

For instance, my daughter Michelle is a talented musician. She played the piano for 10 years and the alto-saxophone during high school. But when I asked her if she had a passion for music, her answer was surprising: "Not really, but I do enjoy it," Michelle said matter-of-factly. You know what? I never heard her play the saxophone after high school. She played the piano a couple of times during one summer because her friend asked her to play for fun, but that's it. Michelle moved on to pursue other interests during her university studies.

What is a Skill?

Skills are something you do well thanks to hard work, and years of experience and/or training. They are something you acquire after you're born. Typically, skills are things you've learned on the job or in life. They aren't necessarily things you love to do or are extraordinary at, but you can do them.

I vividly recall the nerve-wracking experience of teaching my son how to drive. We ventured to the nearby empty school parking lot on a Sunday afternoon. As Isaac opened the door and sat in the driver's seat, beads of sweat popped up on my forehead; as he drove, my right hand tightly clung to the handle above the window. And you can imagine why I was so nervous: Isaac was swerving within a roundabout! Though he became comfortable around the lot that day, the driving lesson ended with a screech when a stray dog appeared in front of our green Subaru Forester. (And yes, the dog crossed the road unharmed!) Six months later, Isaac did become a skilled, licensed (and proud) driver.

Perhaps a young girl has a very pleasant singing voice. Without vocal training and music theory lessons, though, she may not reach her full potential as a skilled musician who can compose or read sheet music. Thus, there are many opportunities to develop skills that enhance our natural abilities or talents.

Gifts Extravaganza

There is no limit to life's greatest gifts. Maybe you're thinking, "I'm just an ordinary homemaker/cashier/computer programmer/accountant/plumber/engineer/teacher/police officer/etc. I don't have special gifts." If this is your view, I challenge you to be objective and think again.

Life gifts come in countless forms and degrees of intensity. How about the gift of cooking a scrumptious dinner? Or the gift of being a good listener? Living your God-given potential to the fullest is about doing what you enjoy, especially in a stimulating or rewarding environment. Within this environment, you are around people who value and treasure your gifts, talents, and skills. This is why it's important to recognize your life gifts, talents, and skills. Let's review Thomas' example to further elaborate.

Case Study: Thomas

"Find a job you love and you'll never work a day in your life."
–Confucius (551 B.C.–479 B.C.), Chinese philosopher

Thomas, a French-Canadian fluent in both English and French, has a very successful and rewarding career as a human resources manager for a global consulting company. He manages a department of 10 staff members with HR specialists, talent acquisition consultants, payroll and contract administrators, plus training consultants. His department is responsible for hiring the right people, providing effective orientation, processing payroll and benefits, providing training programs to maintain a high-quality workforce, and implementing succession plans.

Now let's say the company wanted to open a satellite office in Quebec; they would need a qualified French-speaking HR manager to recruit key positions. Would Thomas be a good fit for that role? Definitely! Thomas enjoys meeting new people (which is his life gift). He has more than 10 years of progressive experience in HR, which is considered to be his acquired skill. His language ability, also known as his talent to speak fluent French, would serve him well when communicating in French.

In the following diagram, three circles intersect; in this intersection, you are at your most productive zone, which is your niche. So let's apply this to a career-oriented situation: you are most fulfilled when you use your life gifts on the job, along with your trained skills and developed talents. For homemakers or people who aren't active in the workforce, you feel most pleased when engaging in enjoyable activities, doing them well and with ease.

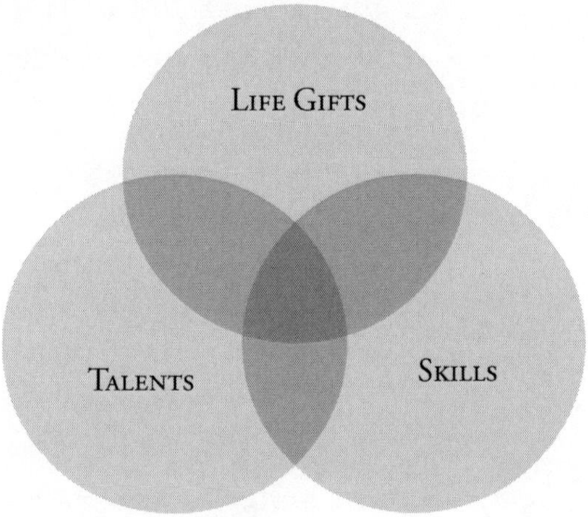

My cousin's husband, Mel, has been working for the U.S. government for over 40 years as a procurement specialist. He is approaching 70, yet he still goes to work happily every day. When he's asked about his retirement plans, he jokingly says, "Maybe in five years." Mel loves his job, his department treasures his expertise and he finds joy in the contract negotiation process, which makes going to work even more enjoyable for him.

Similar to Mel, some people plan to continue working for as long as they can because they enjoy operating in their most productive zone. Or instead, you may choose to engage in lifelong service as Christ followers, volunteering your time locally or abroad. Finding the right fit and doing what you love is invigorating to you and to the people you serve.

Your Turn

Here, you have an opportunity to describe your own gifts, talents, and skills; this will be useful for considering your current job assignment, second career, volunteer opportunities, or future studies. Fill in the blank table below and then look for common elements that appear in all three columns. These common areas are where your life gifts, talents, and skills intersect. This means you have put in an effort to further develop an ability—an ability that you have a natural bent in. You have also mastered that skill and you can exercise it with ease, especially since you are talented in that task. In this case, the outcome of what you do tends to be satisfying. After you have filled in the table, you can also determine if you have any under-developed life gifts, talents, or skills. As an example, you could be an effective teacher who sings like Gordon Lightfoot and cooks authentic Greek dishes comparable to fancy restaurants in Athens.

Life Gifts	**Talents**	**Acquired Skills**
e.g. Singing	*e.g. Teaching*	*e.g. Cooking*

DIFFERING GIFTS

Maybe you're not sure if you have gifts. As a child, you might've been told that you were different, or your gifts were under-valued. I know a family headed by a couple (let's call them Doris and Jim). Doris and Jim are hard-working, currently owning and operating a restaurant. They have three lovely children. Doris is very outgoing and she cooperates well with customers, suppliers, and restaurant helpers. On the other hand, Jim is quiet; he cooks, does all the maintenance work, and he seldom complains.

One day, I visited the family and noticed how their teenage daughter Jennifer was quietly studying away. As I casually asked about Jennifer, Doris started telling me how she's concerned about Jennifer being too passive and introverted. "All she does is bury herself in books and write useless stories," Doris protested.

Jennifer is a writer. She is creative and imaginative. Her mind has a whole universe of characters that laugh, cry, win, lose, love, and hate. Her writings are full of adventures and fantasies. Not everyone can write stories like Jennifer. This is her special gift! Yet, Doris does not recognize it as such. Rather, she worries about her daughter. Doris has the social life gifts of being friendly and outgoing, and having the ability to engage strangers in lively conversations. To be able to craft intricate tales of characters with suspense, mystery, and romance takes sensitivity, creativity, imagination, and persistence. Jennifer has artistic life gifts that make her shine as a writer.

Some of you may find it difficult to detect your life gifts; or maybe you're unsure if they even are life gifts. Perhaps you were trained to perform certain traits well. Or you're confused because you have diverse interests and you're unsure if they are gifts from God. There is a very well developed theory that has led many people into fulfilling careers. This is the tool you will use to discover and validate your list of life gifts.

A Framework for Discovering Life Gifts

In the 1950s, American psychologist Dr. John L. Holland developed a theory on careers and vocational choices, based on a set of interest types. Also known as the Holland Codes,[45] these six interest types are referred to as RIASEC: Realistic, Investigative, Artistic, Social, Enterprising, and Conventional (see following diagram).

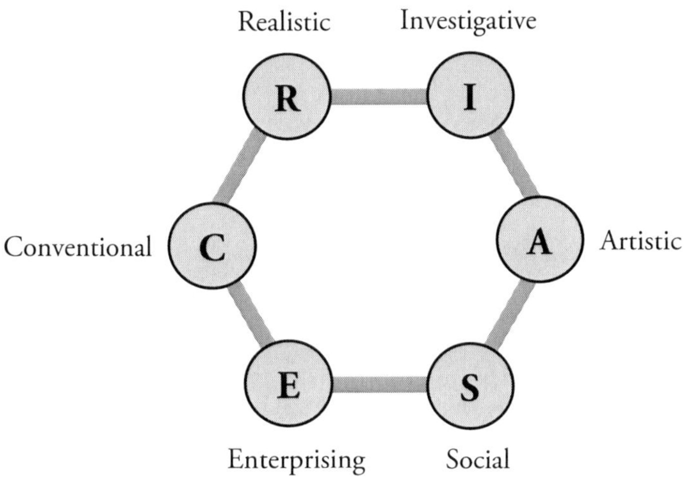

So you might be thinking, "I'm going to retire or I'm already retired—why should I care about a career-based theory?" Well, here's why: Holland's theory presents insights on your interests, pointing you to the direction of your natural bent. Expanding on Holland's theory, Jane Kise, David Stark and Sandra Kreb Hirsh, the authors of *Lifekeys: Discover Who You Are*, have observed that people's life gifts are often derived from their interests.[46] It seems intuitive that we gravitate towards work that we like and perform well.

> Ultimately, your career development is much more than the jobs you pursue—it is about how you want to live your life.
> –Canadian Career Development Foundation

You can evaluate whether you've been operating within or outside your life gifts, and then make any adjustments to fully utilize your life gifts in the future. Find the right fit by targeting a volunteer role or choosing an organization to work for that aligns with your gifts. With that, let's expand on RIASEC. As you review the general description of each interest area, check off any life gifts that apply to you.

Realistic Interests

Realistic people are "doers" who are good at fixing or repairing things. They're practical, matter-of-fact, emotionally stable, reliable, modest, adept at avoiding attention, and they enjoy activities that involve physical risks.

Associated Life Gifts for Realistic Doers

Mechanical aptitude

- They prefer practical, hands-on problems and solutions.

Physical coordination and taking physical risks

- They like athletic activities and skilled trades. They're attracted to activities like piloting, skydiving, etc.

Emotional stability and reliability

- They're able to remain objective and steady in a crisis.

Investigative Interests

Investigative people are "thinkers" who are curious, rational, introspective and perhaps reserved; they're independent and self-motivated, original and creative, scholarly and intellectual, and motivated to find out how and why.

Associated Life Gifts for Investigative Thinkers

Inventing, researching, and conceptualizing

- They enjoy analyzing, exploring, and producing technical, scientific or theoretical-related outcomes.

Solving complex problems, synthesizing information, and theorizing

- They enjoy challenges and finding solutions to difficult issues through logic, analysis, etc.

Technological aptitude

- They enjoy dealing with new technologies. They like to find ways to optimize system performance.

Artistic Interests

Artistic people are creatively or musically talented innovators; they're non-conformists and value the importance of self-expression. They are unstructured, flexible, original, free-spirited, and imaginative; they have an aesthetic flair and are motivated by bursts of inspiration; they are adept at studying or learning languages and possess verbal and linguistic skills.

Associated Life Gifts for Artistic Innovators

Writing or reporting

- They have the ability to communicate effectively through written works, reporting, or technical writing.

Musical or creative expression

- They enjoy activities that involve acting, broadcasting, song writing, dancing, music, painting, etc.; or they exercise creative designs through colors and clothing.

Creative problem-solving

- If they do not consider themselves to be artists, they enjoy the creative aspects of certain professions such as attorneys, research librarians, etc.

Social Interests

Social people are kind and generous helpers; they're friendly and cheerful and good listeners; they are cooperative, supportive, and care for the well-being of others.

Associated Life Gifts for Sociable Helpers

Teaching, counseling, coaching, facilitating

- They encourage others, as well as promote learning and personal development.

Working with others

- They enjoy human interactions and often offer service to others.

Empathy or sensitivity in evaluating human behaviors

- They're aware of other people's feelings and they can adjust their behaviors and respond accordingly. They are gifted at detecting people's motives.

Enterprising Interests

Enterprising people are natural leaders with the ability to influence others; they're optimistic, witty, self-confident, competitive, ambitious, and comfortable taking risks.

Associated Life Gifts for Enterprising Leaders

Public speaking, persuading

- They enjoy outreaching, driving things and/or ideas forward.

Selling, taking action, and being adventurous

- They enjoy entrepreneurial pursuits, sales or marketing, running for political offices, financial planning, and networking.

Managing, negotiating

- They enjoy starting and implementing projects or business ventures.

Conventional Interests

Conventionalists are organizers who are practical, methodical, efficient, and orderly; they're responsible, dependable, conscientious, content, and careful; they prefer structure and routines, and are comfortable and accurate with details.

Associated Life Gifts for Conventionalist Organizers

Managing tasks and time; setting priorities

- They're able to meet goals and deadlines, and conform to procedures and guidelines.

Appraising and categorizing

- They're capable of accurately assessing investment or business opportunities, and providing data in systematic formats.

Perseverance and stewardship

- o They are dependable and conservative in handling money, information, and people.

Holland Codes: Take Note

Some people feel that only one interest type describes their work preference; others find that a blend of two or three types suits them. For example, Randy is a highly ingenious individual and enjoys work using out-of-the-box thinking and autonomy; he is Artistic. Randy is now semi-retired, working as a marketing design consultant for fundraising projects. He enjoys his job because he loves being around people who are unconventional and full of ideas. So it makes sense to say that Artistic people are attracted to making friends and working with other Artistic people. When people with the same interest work together, they create a work environment that fits their type.

While Randy's wife, Cecilia, admires his creative flair, she has strong Conventional and Realistic life gifts. Cecilia works as a part-time nurse in a civic hospital and babysits her granddaughter twice a week. Being able to follow routines well and stay organized makes Cecilia a valuable team member and a superb homemaker.

Cecilia's life gifts relate to another part of Holland's theory: there are more similarities between neighboring interest types. Conventionalists have more in common with Realists and Enterprisers than people with Artistic interests. (And if you take a look at the RIASEC diagram again, you'll notice how the Artistic type is on the opposite side of the hexagon.) Accordingly, being a nurse in a hospital suits Cecilia's interests. She thrives in a busy environment and she can relate to other nurses and therapists on the job. Grand-parenting brings in another dimension of fulfillment since Cecilia, being a Realist, loves outdoor activities. She enjoys taking her granddaughter skating, cycling, and swimming.

Your Next Steps

You can do what you love no matter your age. As mentioned before, discovering your unique life gifts is the first step in figuring out your life purpose. From the life gift checklist you just read, pick your top three gifts and rank them below.

Summarize your responses, accept these gifts with thankfulness, and savor the richness that is given you by the majestic Creator. If you're unable to land on a specific gift after reading each description, you can write down the general interest areas for now.

I enjoy exercising these gifts; I am naturally good with these gifts; I have been using or dreamed about using these gifts. My top three life gifts are:

1) ________________. This belongs to the ______________ (insert RIASEC interest) type.

2) ________________. This belongs to the ______________ (insert RIASEC interest) type.

3) ________________. This belongs to the ______________ (insert RIASEC interest) type.

Picture yourself embracing and relishing these gifts. What do you see? Review your responses; in the empty box below, describe how you would use your gifts. Or if you'd like, draw a diagram or create a dream board. (With a dream board, you would cut and paste images from magazines or newspapers.)

Example of My Life Gift Narrative:

My top life gifts are a blend of Enterprising, Conventional, and Artistic interests. I love to express my ideas and emotions by singing and writing and through public speaking. I enjoy working independently. I am detail-oriented when managing resources and organizing information. I love managing complex projects by breaking them down, analyzing issues through various perspectives, and delivering results to satisfy stakeholders' requirements. I am motivated to inspire others and help them adopt new ideas and skills.

Your Turn:
This is my life gift narrative/diagram/dream board

Spiritual Gifts

God has given each of you a gift from his great variety of spiritual gifts. Use them well to serve one another.
–1 Peter 4:10, NLT

Spiritual gifts are supernatural abilities God sovereignly bestows to His followers to serve the needs of the church. Apostle Paul touched on spiritual gifts through a few passages in the New Testament (1 Corinthians 12, Romans 12, 1 Peter 4, Ephesians 4). In 1 Corinthians 12:1, Apostle Paul warns Christians not to be ignorant about spiritual gifts.

Spiritual gifts are supernatural abilities God sovereignly bestows to His followers to serve the needs of the church.

From the above passages, we can observe the five characteristics of spiritual gifts: first, each believer is given at least one gift from the Holy Spirit. Secondly, the motive of a spiritual gift is expressed with a serving attitude to strengthen the body of Christ. Thirdly, the owner of a spiritual gift is God; the person exercising the gift is drawing from God's strength rather than his or her own. Fourthly, God's grace is disbursed through various spiritual gifts, which are based on speaking His word or helping others. Lastly, when a spiritual gift is expressed, it gives God the glory and honor through Jesus Christ.

That said, spiritual gifts and life gifts might overlap. However, life gifts have a wide range of applications, whereas spiritual gifts carry out God's purposes. For example, many people are good teachers or administrators. Their abilities are God-given, whether people recognize this or not. But they are not considered to be spiritual gifts unless they are applied as service to glorify God and they are expressed to strengthen faith.

Peter Wagner, pastor and author of *Discover Your Spiritual Gifts*, encourages Christians to discover the gifts the Holy Spirit has given us. "What a privilege it is to dream God's dreams!"[47] exclaims Wagner. That's why he advises us to practice our life gifts in our local church.

> If you don't know about spiritual gifts, you may well miss out on God's best plan for your personal life.
> –Peter Wagner

Discerning one's spiritual gifts requires an in-depth study of scriptures and inspiration from the Holy Spirit. It's important to identify our spiritual gifts so that we can exercise them to expand God's kingdom. Here is a summary of the spiritual gifts mentioned in the four passages:[48]

1. *Administration* (refer to 1 Corinthians 12:28; Luke 14:28–30; Acts 6:1–7)

Special ability to identify immediate and long-term goals for certain ministerial work; to create effective plans that lead to the successful accomplishment of those goals.

2. *Apostleship* (refer to 1 Corinthians 12:28; Luke 6:12–13; Ephesians 2:20)
Special abilities to minister to different cultures, start new churches, or establish foundational governance structure to promote the spiritual growth of believers and expand church outreach.

3. *Distinguishing between spirits* (refer to 1 Corinthians 12:10; Matthew 16:21–23; Acts 5:1–11; 1 John 4:1–6)
Special ability to confidently differentiate whether certain behaviors (claimed to be of God) are from the divine, human level, or satanic realms.

4. *Exhortation* (refer to Roman 12:8; Acts 14:22; 1 Timothy 4:13; Hebrews 10:25)
Special ability to bring encouragement to the Body of Christ effectively, through words of comfort, consolation, and wise counsel.

5. *Faith* (refer to 1 Corinthians 12:9; Romans 4:18–21; Hebrews 11)
Special ability to confidently distinguish the will and purpose of God toward His future work.

6. *Generosity* (refer to Roman 12:8; Mark 12:41–44; 2 Corinthians 8:1–7)
Special ability to contribute material resources cheerfully and abundantly, above the tithes and offerings expected from believers.

7. *Healing* (refer to 1 Corinthians 12:9; Acts 3:1–10; 5:12–16)
Special ability to cure diseases and restore health through the power of God.

8. *Being helpful* (refer to 1 Corinthians 12:28; Mark 15:40–41; Luke 8:2–3; Romans 16:1–2)
Special ability to offer their talents to enrich the lives of other believers, enabling them to increase the effectiveness of their spiritual gifts. (A person who has the gift of helping usually supports one individual rather than a whole project or ministry area.)

9. *Hospitality* (refer to Romans 12:9–13; Acts 16:14–15)
Special ability to extend a warm welcome or provide an open house for those who need food and board.

10. *Interpreting tongues* (refer to 1 Corinthians 12:10, 30; 14:13–14, 26–28)
Special ability to translate a message spoken by someone in tongues (the language one has never learned).

11. *Knowledge* (refer to 1 Corinthians 12:8; Colossians 2:2–3; 2 Corinthians 11:6)
Special ability to discover, learn, accumulate, analyze, and clarify information and ideas that benefit the well-being of the Body of Christ.

12. *Leadership* (refer to Roman 12:8; Luke 9:51; Acts 15:7–11; 1 Timothy 5:17; Hebrews 13:17)
Special ability to set future goals according to God's purpose; to guide others to accomplish those goals to bring glory to God.

13. *Mercy* (refer to Roman 12:8; Matthew 20:29–34; 25:34–40; Mark 9:41)
Special ability to feel empathy and compassion to those who suffer hardship, and to bring comfort and relief through Christ's love.

14. *Miraculous powers* (refer to 1 Corinthians 12:10, 28; Romans 15:18–19; Acts 9:36–42)
Special ability to perform supernatural acts through the power of God.

15. *Pastor* (refer to Ephesians 4:11–13; John 10:1–18; 1 Timothy 3:1–7; 1 Peter 5:1–3)
Special ability to assume the long-term responsibility to support believers in their spiritual well-being.

16. *Prophecy* (refer to 1 Corinthians 12:10; Romans 12:6; Acts 15:32, 21:9–11; Ephesians 4:11–13)
Special ability to receive and communicate the message of God through a divine utterance.

17. *Service* (refer to Romans 12:7; Acts 6:1–7; 2 Timothy 1:16–18; Titus 3:14)
Special ability to recognize and apply resources to fulfill unmet needs that relate to God's work. (A person who has the gift of service usually provides support to a project, a church, or a ministry area).

18. *Teaching* (refer to Romans 12:7; 1 Corinthians 12:28; Acts 18:24–28, 20:20–21; Ephesians 4:11–13)
Special ability to communicate information relevant to the health and ministry of the Body of Christ for others to learn.

19. Tongues (or speaking in tongues) (refer to 1 Corinthians 12:10, 28; 14:13–19; Mark 16:17; Acts 2:1–13; 10:44–46)
Special ability to speak to God in a language that was never learned, or to receive and communicate a divine message from God to His people in a language that was never learned.

20. Wisdom (refer to 1 Corinthians 12:8, 2:1–13; 2 Peter 3:15–16)
Special ability to discern the mind of the Holy Spirit, and receive insight to apply this knowledge towards specific needs of the Body of Christ.

Some Bible scholars suggest other spiritual gifts that are mentioned in other New Testament passages. These include the gifts of intercession, celibacy, deliverance, evangelism, leading worship, martyrdom, mission, and voluntary poverty.

As you study the referenced scripture passages and review the above spiritual gifts, read over the next phrases. Then check off the one that applies to you. This will help you reflect on how you have or have not been applying your spiritual gifts in expanding God's kingdom or building other believers in their faith.

❑ I understand that I have the gift of ________________ because ____.

❑ I don't know if I possess any spiritual gifts. I need to pray and study the scriptures more to understand this topic further.

❑ I am not sure if I know my spiritual gifts. I need to review other resources and tools in order to discover my gifts.

The Bible is clear on the expectation that believers are to engage in lifelong service and commitment in supporting the local church and global mission fields. Discern your God-given spiritual gift(s), and use it for His glory.

Summary

You are indeed special. I congratulate you if you have a firm understanding of your life gifts: what interests you, what comes naturally to you, the areas you excel in, your spiritual gift and, in particular, specific abilities God has given you for extending His kingdom. But if you're struggling in defining your gifts, you can always consult your pastor or a career counselor. Knowing your life gifts prepares you to succeed in your next phase of life. Other people will benefit from your gifts, as it is God's desire for you and me to be the light and salt of this world, to make an impact. In the next chapter, you will embark further into your self-discovery journey. You will identify your personality type, your strengths and weaknesses, and your emotional needs.

> You already have every characteristic necessary for success if you recognize, claim, develop and use them.
> –Zig Ziglar, author, motivational speaker, personal development guru

seven

IDENTIFYING YOUR PERSONALITY, STRENGTHS AND WEAKNESSES

"For you created my inmost being;
you knit me together in my mother's womb.
I praise you because I am fearfully and wonderfully made;
your works are wonderful, I know that full well."
Psalm 139:13–14

"Keep your feet on the ground, but let your heart soar as high as it will.
Refuse to be average or to surrender to the chill of your spiritual environment."
–A.W. Tozer (1897–1963), pastor, author

"Live out of your imagination instead of out of your memory."
–Les Brown, America Motivational speaker, author

BLUE EYES, BLACK HAIR, FRECKLES, ROUND SHOULDERS, SKINNY arms or long legs—these are all features you can see when you meet someone. But how would you describe a person's temperament? By temperament, I am referring to behavioral tendencies and a natural disposition. Is a person animated, spontaneous, persuasive, and daring? Or is he sensitive, orderly, easygoing, and content?

> Temperament is the combination of inborn traits that subconsciously affects all our behavior.
> –Tim LaHaye, author of *Spirit-Controlled Temperament*

Psychologists have learned that people are born with traits that form our basic personalities. And this is so true! In fact, four of my former colleagues remind me of these different personalities. Maybe you can relate to some of their special traits.

Popular Sandra

Sandra is charming, bubbly, creative, outgoing, and well-liked. Her motto in life is "fun and friends." She spends many hours on social media, keeping up with her network list of more than 300 friends. Being trendy and attractive is very important to Sandra. Her pastime includes parties and it's no surprise that she is the life of each party with loud, amusing, and colorful stories.

On weekends, Sandra enjoys shopping, though she may not always remember when her credit card payment is overdue. At work, you might find her spending too much time chatting with the people around her and missing a few deadlines. Plus, she's often late for meetings, frequently dealing with last-minute preparations, or getting distracted when she runs into old friends.

Powerful Chris

Chris is a natural-born leader and talented in encouraging people to complete tasks. He knows what he wants in life and he is quick to act on any opportunity that arises. Chris takes pride in his work as a marketing director. Since he's determined and accustomed to being in charge, he sometimes finds himself making decisions for others or finishing other people's sentences.

Unlike Sandra, Chris only enjoys parties that serve a particular purpose. He thinks most wild parties are a waste of time, except for the odd networking function, where he can connect with potential employers or customers.

In the office, Chris frequently works overtime, burying himself in projects. He's dependable and seldom misses deadlines. Chris is goal-oriented and, at times, may appear rude when he makes his point. He could learn to be more tactful when dealing with his peers or subordinates, especially when he's under stress.

Perfect Melissa

Melissa is a quiet, conscientious, sensitive middle-age woman, with a deep appreciation for the arts. As a research specialist, she's knowledgeable about health, wellness, and nutrition. She relies on and adheres to her schedule and uses sticky-note reminders, checklists, and charts to stay organized.

Melissa arranges her workspace and home neatly and meticulously, clean and clutter-free. In her spare time, she writes stories, enjoys oil paintings, and tends to her well-landscaped garden. On the job, she prefers working alone rather than with groups. Melissa holds a high standard for her duties and she will work on a task until she believes it's perfect.

Peaceful Phil

Phil is easygoing, laid back, and adaptable when he's handling different personalities. His friends enjoy his company because he's pleasant, cooperative, and patient; he can get along with almost everybody.

Phil has high moral standards and lives by his principles. He can be indecisive at times. But once Phil makes up his mind, he stands by his decision. He has a mellow disposition and is emotionally stable, without exhibiting extreme highs and lows most of the time.

During his downtime, Phil loves to relax at home on his recliner, watching his favorite sport shows on The Sports Network (TSN).

On the job, Phil is a reliable and supportive team member in the engineering department. He works on his assignments diligently and produces consistent outputs. His contribution in the office is valued, though he doesn't crave personal credit and attention from his colleagues. In conflicting situations, Phil tries to avoid confrontation at all costs.

His Way, Her Way

Surely, you have come across people who are like Popular Sandra, Powerful Chris, Perfect Melissa, and Peaceful Phil. In fact, these individuals have characteristics from four basic personality patterns. Recognizing these patterns will help you understand why people behave the way they do, why they approach life differently, and why some people are not "just like me."

Certain characteristics form our basic temperaments. In the early stages of my marriage, I struggled to understand why my husband behaved the way he did, especially after some serious arguments. Many times, I thought he was just outright barbarous and that he deliberately made me upset by acting weird! I once wondered why someone would spend four hours in front of the TV on a Saturday afternoon. For me, the weekend meant personal productivity galore: I would make a to-do list at the beginning of the week to maximize my day off, with tasks like paying the bills, testing a new eatery, getting a haircut, and rearranging the kitchen cabinet. Even now if I watch TV, I would keep myself busy at the same time by knitting or polishing my shoes!

It's liberating to know that God created us as unique individuals. If someone has a different outlook, it should not be viewed as a wrong way of thinking. My husband prefers to relax during his day off, whereas I like to keep busy. Things still get done by the end of the day. We've been married for 30 years now. He still enjoys his TV shows while I hardly know which remote to use! Someone asked me what the secret to our marriage was. I simply replied, "We are attracted to our strengths and we learned to be graceful about each other's weaknesses."

Nonetheless, identifying personalities is not about boxing people into stereotypes; it's about living in harmony with others, despite our differences. Grasping your unique blend of temperaments will help you to strategically live your best. So generally speaking, here are the reasons it's never too late to learn about our personality:

...identifying personalities is not about... stereotypes; it's about living in harmony with others, despite our differences. Grasping your unique blend of temperaments will help you to...live your best.

1. You'll fall in love with yourself

If you're like me, you may be critical about yourself sometimes. I had a counseling client once reveal how she disliked being shy. In fact, she thought she had a bad personality! We explored her complete personality package and she became amazed at the superior qualities she possessed as a musician. We agreed that being shy was not a negative trait; really, this meant she preferred processing her thoughts internally rather than speaking her mind. But my client realized that she needed to learn how to openly share her feelings during necessary times. As a result, she took assertive communication courses. By understanding her personality further, she no longer compares her traits with others and she embraces her individuality.

2. You'll be a better friend

Understanding different personalities helps you see why you get along with some people and not others. From my experience, this has allowed me to appreciate everyone around me (and myself) so much better. Some time ago, I had a co-worker I avoided like the plague. He was talkative, brassy, and always joking around instead of getting the work done. Looking back, I was silly to discount his charming personality and his special ability to motivate the team in achieving a common goal. If I have a chance to work with him again, I would ask about his weekend stories. Many times, the biggest reward in life is sharing special moments with someone you care about. True friendship goes a long way.

3. You will strengthen your strengths

No matter your life stage, understanding your personality challenges you to grow to become a better person. Awareness of our strengths motivates us to achieve something greater. Recognizing our weaknesses creates opportunities for learning and self-improvement.

For my friend—let's call him Kenneth, an insight into various temperaments helped him understand the breaking point in his marriage. During a personality study offered by his church, Kenneth realized that conflict stemmed from personality differences between his ex-wife and himself, especially when it came to finances. He was organized, detail-oriented in budgeting, and a careful shopper. His ex-wife, on the other hand, loved shopping, didn't keep record of her spending, forgot where she kept credit card statements, and frequently missed bill payment deadlines.

Kenneth just assumed that financial management was common sense and everyone should be able to keep tabs on income versus expense. He told me that if he had known his ex-wife's personality flaws beforehand, he would've handled the family budget. Plus, he would have confronted her about irresponsible spending rather than allowing the issue to fester. Now that he's aware of his weaknesses, Kenneth is more assertive and expresses his negative feelings rather than letting resentment build up. Kenneth currently has a new girlfriend and he is enjoying his new relationship.

PERSONALITIES 101

It's time to place Popular Sandra, Powerful Chris, Perfect Melissa, and Peaceful Phil into a theoretical setting. Marita Littauer, author of

Wired That Way, suggests that each person has a dominant personality, with the affinity of having a secondary one. Littauer summarizes the characteristics, strengths, weaknesses, and emotional needs of four basic personalities:[49]

Popular Sanguines

- They tend to speak loudly.
- They prefer to dress in attractive clothes with bold colors.
- They like telling stories and they don't mind being center stage.
- They usually have a cluttered personal space.
- Acceptance from others is important to them.
- Strengths: naturally curious, keen and lively, effortlessly make friends.
- Weaknesses: tend to be egotistic, undisciplined, erratic and scatterbrained.

Powerful Cholerics

- They speak with confidence and conviction.
- In terms of style, they choose function over fashion.
- They bring positive energy and excitement; they bring negative stress and tension.
- They tend to be heavy-footed, focused, intense, and "in your face."
- They need to feel appreciated by others.
- Strengths: radiate confidence, goal-oriented, excel in leadership and organization.
- Weaknesses: tend to be insensitive, argumentative, may be headstrong, have a hard time apologizing.

Perfect Melancholies

- They tend to talk softly.
- They dress in traditional styles and colors, and prefer to buy clothes with lasting value.

- They prefer silence and being alone.
- They usually keep their personal space orderly.
- They need support from others.
- Strengths: sensitive to other people's feelings; proficient with charts, graphs and lists; concerned about others.
- Weaknesses: tend to be irritable and unhappy, may spend excessive amount of time planning, difficult to satisfy, suspicious of other people's intentions.

Peaceful Phlegmatics

- They are adaptable and diplomatic.
- They can remain calm and collected.
- They dress for comfort rather than fashion.
- They convey a relaxed body language (i.e. they seem to be flowing when they walk, and prefer to lie down instead of sitting upright).
- They need to feel respected by others.
- Strengths: good listeners, inoffensive, easygoing, usually relaxed.
- Weaknesses: can be indecisive but they tend to stick to their decision once it's made; lack motivation, sluggish, withdrawn.

Mix and Match

Like I explained earlier, you may feel like you relate to one personality pattern while having characteristics from another. Some of these personality types blend well—and some do not. Florence Littauer explains this concept further in her book *Personality Plus* as two types of blends: natural and complementary.[50]

Natural Blend

Equivalent to how a hand fits a glove, some personality types intuitively blend well. There are commonalities and strong ties between both sets of their traits. Sanguines and Cholerics are both extroverts. People and events invigorate Sanguines, while Cholerics are energized by goals and actions. Individuals with Sanguine-Choleric blend disposition have great potential to be visionary leaders. They also have the ability to rally people for a cause while carrying an optimistic outlook. If they do not watch their limits, though, they may be candidates for burnouts.

On the other hand, Phlegmatics and Melancholies are introverts. Phlegmatics are not necessarily eager about meeting people or attending events; Melancholies prefer discreetness and solitude. Individuals who carry the Phlegmatic-Melancholy blend disposition are likely outstanding teachers or scholars who are careful in organizing information. They're also adept at analytical tasks while maintaining a supportive spirit. However, they may become sluggish if they procrastinate for too long.

Complementary Blend

My friend loves hot and spicy food, so it's no surprise that Pad Thai is her favorite dinner. On top of that, she orders sweet chilli sauce! She says the sweet chilli sauce rounds off the salty, gingery, spicy, tangy flavors of the Pad Thai noodles. This mishmash fits well together, creating a perfectly sensational dish.

The complementary personality blend works like Pad Thai with sweet chilli sauce (or wine and cheese, for those of you who aren't fans of spicy noodles). Unlike natural blending, complementary blending enhances or intensifies traits from each personality.

In a positive sense, people with the Choleric-Melancholy combination have the potential to be high achievers, as they're driven by purpose and perfection. They are persistent and hard-working; they persevere through ups and downs and experience breakthrough successes. In a negative sense, people with this combination can become critical and overly sensitive if they take themselves to the extremes.

The Sanguine-Phlegmatic blend consists of well-liked, diplomatic, and joyful people. They make the best of friends because they are easygoing and fun. On the downside, they may lack motivation, become easily distracted, and display carelessness in their finances.

Personalities in Action

Popular Sanguine

Powerful Choleric

Peaceful Phlegmatic

Perfect Melancholy

Clashing Temperaments

Is it possible to have combinations of Sanguine-Melancholy or Choleric-Phlegmatic? Look over the "Personalities in Action" sketches. Now, look at their diagonal positions—they are opposites. So if you knew yourself to be a Sanguine-Melancholy, would it make sense to say that you tend to speak loudly and softly? Consequently, it is unusual to have these personality combinations. But if you do see yourself with a Sanguine-Melancholy or Choleric-Phlegmatic blend, there may be underlying factors. These factors cause confusion between how you see your temperaments and how you want to be perceived.

In *Wired That Way*, Marita Littauer examines masking, which denotes behaviors that people have unintentionally taken on. This is for the purpose of surviving or conforming to an environment. "Usually this occurs in childhood," writes Littauer, explaining how people originally use masking to "make their parents happy or to make their parents like them better."[51]

For that reason, masking creates an inner struggle, manifesting into a person's stress, exhaustion, or nervousness. Unfortunately, the cause of this turmoil is not distinguishable, as the mask is on a subliminal level.

NOTE: It is beyond the scope of this book to elaborate on factors related to personality masking. If you have an interest on this subject, consult a mental health professional, such as an experienced counselor or psychologist, who has been trained in personality theories.

We don't have to be psychologists to appreciate natural personality makeups. The key to understanding temperaments is to increase our awareness of who we are at the root of our design, rather than how we want to be perceived. My friend Elaine studied these personalities with me and revealed a painful story.

> The key to understanding temperaments is to increase our awareness of who we are at the root of our design, rather than how we want to be perceived.

Growing up, she had to live as a compliant child, unconsciously suppressing her Sanguine traits to please her overbearing, Melancholy mother. Elaine remembered being punished for laughing loudly at the dinner table. Her mother did not allow her to dress in colorful clothes, either. During Elaine's teen years, social events were strictly forbidden. She felt miserable most of the time, yet she complied because upsetting her mom would risk further rejection.

Acceptance from others is vital to Elaine. When she first learned about the personalities, she checked off traits that belonged to Melancholy, Sanguine, and a few from Choleric. As mentioned earlier, this is an unusual combination. But take a look at Elaine's suppressive past—see why she related to opposites? If I told you now that Elaine is in her 60s and that she is a lively, funny public speaker, with sparkly eyes as she talks, how would you describe her real personality?

Who Am I?

Elaine was overjoyed when she began acting like her free, true self. It was like a veil lifted from her when she accepted the way God designed her to be. So now it's your turn to reflect on your strengths, weaknesses, and emotional needs. You can live your finest by excelling in what you're already endowed with. In turn, this will help you select new careers or volunteer opportunities that are suitable for your next phase of life.

Review the following list and check off the qualities that describe you. Base your answers on *your* view of yourself or *your* natural preference, not how you want others to see you.

Another way to approach this exercise is to read each line aloud and listen to your response. If you immediately nod or say "yes," then check off the box. If you immediately reply "no," simply move on.

Key Strengths

- ❑ I am naturally curious
- ❑ I possess lots of energy and I am highly enthusiastic about people and events

- ❑ I make friends easily
- ❑ I am animated and love to tell stories
- ❑ I am goal-oriented and firm
- ❑ I am a high achiever
- ❑ I love to get things done and bring closure to unfinished projects
- ❑ I am a leader at home, in school, and/or in organizations
- ❑ I am sensitive and detail-oriented
- ❑ I am highly organized and prefer using charts, graphs, and checklists
- ❑ I have a deep concern for others
- ❑ I am a good listener and a peacemaker
- ❑ I am steadfast in my belief
- ❑ I am patient, easygoing, and relaxed
- ❑ I am generally content with life
- ❑ I am emotionally stable

Key Weaknesses

- ❑ I tend to be self-centered
- ❑ I can't complete tasks because I get distracted by talking too much
- ❑ I am forgetful and easily distracted
- ❑ I appear to be blunt, angry, impatient, or too serious
- ❑ I come across as rude, without tact, or "in your face"
- ❑ I am too impulsive and intimidating to others
- ❑ I am too much of a perfectionist and critical of others
- ❑ I am often moody and depressed
- ❑ When I'm stressed, I may become obsessive over certain behaviors (e.g. binge eating, being overly controlling, etc.)
- ❑ I have a hard time making decisions, but once I make a decision, I tend to stick to it
- ❑ I lack a sense of direction to advance in life
- ❑ I lack the motivation to do something out of my comfort zone

- ❑ I am unadventurous or dull
- ❑ I procrastinate because I do not realize my deadline is looming
- ❑ I procrastinate because I dread anything that seems like work
- ❑ I procrastinate because I'm committed to more than I can handle
- ❑ I procrastinate because I spend too much time perfecting details

Emotional Needs

- ❑ I desire attention and affection
- ❑ I need to feel accepted
- ❑ I like to be around people
- ❑ I need to feel in control
- ❑ I need to feel challenged
- ❑ I value loyalty
- ❑ I need to feel appreciated for my good work
- ❑ I may become wary of others due to my sensitive nature
- ❑ I need my space and quiet time
- ❑ I need support from others
- ❑ Maintaining self-worth is important to me
- ❑ I am most afraid of having to deal with personal conflicts
- ❑ I prefer a stress-free environment

Temperament Inventory

The next part of this exercise builds your profile, which will describe who you are. You will also be identifying opportunities for maximizing your strengths, minimizing your weaknesses, and finding healthy ways to satisfy your emotional needs.

Write your responses from the above checklist and focus on your strongest traits or qualities. For instance, if you pick five or more items, concentrate on the ones most significant to you. (Tip: try to zoom in on your top three responses.)

1) Write down the top two or three assets you can use to live out your potential.

Let's say your life goal is to share your faith with people around the world. What you would do is choose the specific strength or strengths that will help you share your faith (e.g. able to make friends easily, possess high energy, etc.).

Which key strengths will help you to live out your best?

*Strengths:*____

2) Let's look at your key weaknesses, which you can view as opportunities for making continuous improvements. Perhaps you tend to be blunt, angry, impatient, or too serious with others. To become more relaxed and patient, you can observe others who are able to tolerate differences—look at how they deal with difficult situations. You can also read jokes and watch comedies for relaxation; learn to laugh at yourself and the silly things you see in life.

Identify one or two key weaknesses you can commit to working on in the near future. These are your growth opportunities.

Weaknesses: ______________________________________

Self-improvement strategies: ___________________________

3) Many people work in jobs that mismatch with their personality and they wonder why they feel burned out after a 40-hour workweek. Pinpointing your emotional needs helps you recognize why you feel a certain way.

For example, John works in a warehouse and his main responsibility is to fulfill customer orders. He reads off the order online, picks and packs the order into a box, creates a shipment label, and passes on the order to the dispatching department for shipping. As a Popular Sanguine, he loves affection and attention from people. His emotional needs are not met while dealing with products, boxes, and forklifts. Which is why John usually hangs out with his buddies after work to help him "recharge."

If you like being around people, consider applying for volunteer roles that involve client interactions. In turn, you may want to avoid volunteer positions that require sitting in an office seven hours a day.

What are your emotional needs?

Emotional Needs: ________________________________

Personal Growth

I am a Powerful Choleric. This means I could probably learn how to soften my strong-headed approach when interacting with others. All the while, I could improve my patience when listening to other opinions. I may feel correct most of the time, but it doesn't mean other views are wrong. Learning to appreciate individuals and applying the right improvement strategies has assisted my personal growth.

As Christians, we can expect God's transforming power to shape us into mature, loving souls that exhibit Godly characteristics. Pastor Tim LaHaye encourages us in his book, *Spirit-Controlled Temperaments,* to refine our temperaments through the Holy Spirit. With our cooperation, God is able to put us through a refinery process. Our strengths can be further improved, while weaknesses can be overcome.[52]

In John 15, Jesus shows us that He is the vine, and we are the branches; God, the Father, is the vinedresser. Through pruning, the branches become stronger and bear much fruit. God prunes us and helps us to bear good fruits as well. The Apostle Paul depicts the qualities of good fruit to be of love, joy, peace, patience, kindness, goodness, faithfulness, gentleness, and self-control (Galatians 5:22–23). Christians are challenged to develop all of those qualities by subjecting themselves to biblical teachings and practicing spiritual disciplines. Whenever we examine our weaknesses, we can invite

God's spirit to empower us to be more Christ-like. We all have room to grow and a special role to fill.

In order to live out our specific roles, God created each of us differently. We need each temperament for the total functioning of the body. Consider what Florence Littauer discusses in *Personality Plus*: think about the Powerful Cholerics—they are the feet. They act with a purpose and accomplish goals. The Perfect Melancholies are the minds. They feel other people's pain, hurt, and joy. The Peaceful Phlegmatics are the hands. They smooth out conflicts and they are peacemakers. The Popular Sanguines are the mouths. They tell stories that brighten up a heavy heart. They are the cheerleaders of the world.[53]

However, when we operate on our own strength without Christ, there will be a lack of coordination in the outcome and no unity of purpose. We need Christ in our lives so that He can orchestrate the functioning of the body parts the way they should be. As we strive to become more like Christ, He has the power to transform us from within. Many people can testify to this truth, including myself.

Claim Your Prize

In the New Testament of the Bible, the Apostle Paul is a distinctive, dynamic character. He transformed from a hostile, obsessive, violent, destructive persecutor of Christians to a loving, passionate, articulate, peace-seeking servant of God. His basic personality traits did not change; however, his awareness of what God desired him to be changed, which is to love God wholeheartedly, love others unconditionally, and spread the good news of Jesus Christ. Allowing the Holy Spirit to work through Paul converted him into a peaceful man.

God created our personalities. If we continue to remain open to the Holy Spirit's shaping of our lives, we can move from dull to polished and from weak to strong.

Forgetting what is behind and straining toward what is ahead, I press on toward the goal to win the prize for which God has called me heavenward in Christ Jesus.
–Philippians 3:13–14

The Apostle Paul encourages us to "press on toward the goal to win the prize." We can't do it alone. But in Christ Jesus we can. Whether you're seeking a second career or a volunteer prospect, consider the serious needs that need to be filled on a local and international basis. People who need your help are the hungry, sick, homeless, abused, oppressed, blind, crippled, drug and alcohol addicts, the illiterate, mentally ill, elderly, and imprisoned; or they are the friendless and lonely.

Glow in the Dark

Here, check off the role (or roles) you're interested in pursuing. Or fill in the blank line for a dream role that best suits your personality. Keep these roles in mind as you plan for volunteerism or a new career for your retirement.

❑ Compassionate caregiver
❑ Creative artist
❑ Dependable administrator
❑ Influential executive
❑ Ingenious scientist
❑ Inspiring teacher
❑ Motivational speaker
❑ Skilled mechanic
❑ Spontaneous performer
❑ Trustworthy guardian
❑ Visionary inventor

____

Summary

Understanding your personality enables you to maximize your strengths, thereby fostering harmony in your relationships. This supports you in becoming a champion in your own race. Get ready to prepare for the last leg of your journey, in which you will climb to new heights and reach for your dreams. Achieve your personal best and finish well—leave a lasting legacy that brings glory to God.

But our citizenship is in heaven. And we eagerly await a Savior from there, the Lord Jesus Christ...will transform our lowly bodies so that they will be like his glorious body.
–Philippians 3:20–21

Do not conform to the pattern of this world, but be transformed by the renewing of your mind. Then you will be able to test and approve what God's will is—his good, pleasing and perfect will.
–Romans 12:2

eight

REVITALIZE YOUR PASSION

"Life is no 'brief candle' to me. It is a … splendid torch which I have got hold of for the moment; and I want to make it burn as brightly as possible before handing it on to future generations."
–George Bernard Shaw (1856–1950), playwright

"Our imagination is the only limit to what we can hope to have in the future."
–Charles F. Kettering, American engineer, inventor

"Teach us to number our days, that we may gain a heart of wisdom."
–Psalm 90:12

OLD AGE IS A GIFT. THE PSALMIST REMINDS US OF THE BREVITY OF life. Discovering your passion is the key to living out your life purpose. Which is why this book highlights how you can get onboard a purposeful and fulfilling life journey—even into old age.

We are encouraged to count our days on earth and to live wisely. We have different gifts, talents, and special interests. We have our distinct calling in life. I no longer want to trade lives with anyone. I treasure who I am, what I have, and what I am to become.

Childhood Dream

Growing up was not easy, financially or emotionally. My parents struggled to provide for their five children, so they experienced much labor and toil. The seven of us lived tightly in a tiny three-bedroom apartment, shared with another family consisting of a couple and their little boy.

Every member of my family had to bring in side income to keep us fed. That meant no extra money for music or art classes. However, my childhood dream was to become a movie star. As I entered my teenage years, singing became the center stage of my free time. Though I wasn't a professional, I continued to sing to entertain myself. I dreamed that one day I would become a pop star.

Years later in 1982, I entered the Hong Kong debut of the *New Talent Singing Contest*, a competition similar to *American Idol* and *Britain's Got Talent*. Among the 3,000 contestants, I was lucky to make it to the semi-final round.

For the inexperienced and insecure performer, standing on a huge red stage in the prestigious Lee Theatre—along with 30 other semi-finalists—was intimidating. On the day of the audition, my makeup made me look too pale, my shoes were uncomfortable (my heels were ridiculously high in the first place!) and my voice was not projecting the way I wanted it to be. But I was there to give it my best shot.

I was eliminated, as expected. On the other hand, everyone eyeing the contest knew who the winner was from the get-go. She had it all: she stood tall, was well-groomed, confident, and adorable. Anita Mui was only 17 at the time and, apparently, had been performing since the age of five. After winning the *New Talent Singing Contest,* Anita remained in the spotlight for nearly 20 years, with international fame and fortune as a major star, singer, and actress. Notably in 1995, Anita co-starred in the action movie *Rumble in the Bronx* with Jackie Chan, which cashed in over $32 million in the U.S. box office. When she was 40, she took everyone by surprise when she was diagnosed with cervical cancer and passed away. Her legend will always remain in my heart.

If Only I Could ...

My dream to become a pop star vaporized as the curtain rolled back at the Lee Theatre. My voyage into stardom never took off. I continued with life—got married, built a career, immigrated to Canada, raised a family, studied part-time, served our church community. For years, I admired Anita's talent, boldness, beauty, style, and her contralto singing voice since the day we shared the stage. Often, I secretly wondered, "Ah, if only I could trade lives with Anita..." I would have performed sold-out concerts around the world. Every household would play my platinum albums and, best of all, I could sing to entertain others to my heart's content.

Ironically, when the media asked Anita if she'd rather be a simple bar singer or a major star, she responded: "If I could, I would choose to be a happy ordinary person."[54] Anita had fame and fortune. She was a trendsetter, a world-renowned performer—yet she was lonely. She was never married and remained single until she died. Unfortunately, Anita did not have a chance to experience "old age" either.

Passion and Purpose

Everyone seems to hold a seed of passion inside his or her soul. Anita's singing and performing arts were developed and recognized over her short lifespan, but she was also known for her avid charity work.

> Everyone seems to hold a seed of passion inside his or her soul.

What are you passionate about? Is it music? Writing? Rescuing stray animals? Social justice? Skydiving? In *Your Personality Tree,* author Florence Littauer highlights her mother-in-law's dream of becoming an opera singer, which followed her into old age. "Mother Littauer" was 85 years old when *Your Personality Tree* was published (1986). Her cognitive functions were no longer coherent and she couldn't talk at all, though the strangest thing happened: a nurse claimed that Mother Littauer continued to sing opera, diligently practicing her scales every day.[55]

Living life to its full potential is about releasing that seed of passion, giving it life, and cultivating it to its full bloom.

Passion persists in our hearts when everything else fades away. It will follow us to the grave. In my case, 30 years later, my dream lives. My passion persists. I still love to sing. Furthermore, my soul leaps, weeps, chants, and cheers through the written words. My writing is a song from my heart. Living life to its full potential is about releasing that seed of passion, giving it life, and cultivating it to its full bloom. Can you relate to the following poem?

Unlived Passion Lives

By Joyce Li

I love to sing.
I love to think.
I love to entertain.
I love to sing and think and entertain.

Who retained in me the passion to sing, think and entertain?
Who ordained in me the days of my life?

He is the one who owns the cattle on a thousand hills.
The one who leads me along the path of righteousness.
The one who quenches my thirst with living water.
His name is to be praised from the rising of the sun to its setting.

By grace, I embrace joy and comfort.
Hardship and pain I endure.
What will be gained without pain?

By faith, I envision glory and wonder.
Victory and hope I enthrone.
What will be missed without hope?

Looking back, traces of your footprints I marveled to view.
Pressing forward, steps of new heights I aspire to climb.
Gracious one, guide me to reflect, reimagine and reinvent.
Give life to the unlived passion through your invisible hand.

To many people, the biggest life regrets are either not getting what they want or getting what they don't. For years, I was unhappy because I was not getting what I wanted in life. My singing career was short-circuited and my stardom goal was crushed.

Serve the LORD *with gladness: come before his presence with singing.*
–Psalm 100:2, KJV

Little did I know that God is most interested in hearing me sing! I can pour my heart out to Him through songs. What a privilege it is to sing unto the Lord with joyful songs and worship Him in response to His goodness! I can do this anytime, anywhere, no matter how old I am. Comparable to lifelong service, God expects believers to worship Him unto old age. Worship is our active expression in response to God's love. I was further reminded to connect my passion in singing to worshipping and serving God.

God is the giver of life. He sets passion in our hearts, which moves us to act. More importantly, we can steer our passion towards a ministry tool, sharing Jesus' love through songs, words, paintings, or deeds.

George Beverly Shea is a fine example of this notion. Shea is a composer, singer, and musical figure in the Billy Graham crusade ministry. Together with Rev. Graham, he has toured the world with their timeless gospel message to presidents, children, the rich and the poor. Born in 1909, he's been singing to testify God's saving grace longer than many people have lived. (On a side note, my favorite hymn by Shea is *I'd Rather Have Jesus*.) At age 102, Shea received the Lifetime Achievement Grammy Award by The Recording Academy in 2011. Now that he's reached 103, he continues to sing to praise the Lord.[56]

PASSIONATE PURSUIT

In Chapter 5, we were reminded of how Joshua trusted God and succeeded Moses as leader of the Israelites. During the same period, Caleb was another faith hero. Instead of perishing in the wilderness, Caleb inherited the land that God promised because he trusted God wholeheartedly. Caleb is highly acclaimed for his passion in following God's will (Numbers 14:24). The Bible describes Caleb as having a "different spirit."

In today's term, I interpret Caleb's stance as being counter-culture. The majority follows what is pleasing to the eyes rather than pursuing eternal values. The media appeals to us in seeking instant gratification rather than adopting habits that yield longer-term benefits. We need to espouse a different spirit to nurture our passion. Perhaps following a less-travelled path, keeping active rather than retreating to leisure living. This may require us to step outside of what feels routine and comfortable. Another baby boomer role model, Cindy Joseph, fits in well to illustrate this point as her boldness and courage inspires many.

Packed with 27 years of experience as a makeup artist in the U.S. fashion and beauty industry, Cindy Joseph challenges age barriers and stereotypes on aging. She started modeling at age 49. Following her passion, Cindy launched her own cosmetic line in her late 50s. Cindy is driven by her "faith that women's perspectives about themselves are changing." She continues to create safe skin care products and cosmetics for women to look and feel their best. She goes for "Pro-age" rather than "Anti-age" by highlighting women's natural looks without masking their wrinkles.

Discover Your Passion

Here's your opportunity to capture your passion on paper. It may be very obvious to you; perhaps you're already living it and, if so, congratulations! For others, it may not be as apparent. Start by reflecting on your childhood dream and your interests. Ask your parents or siblings if they can recall what your favorite activities were when you were young. Look through your personal collections—rediscover the trophies, awards, and mementos you may have kept in your drawers.

As you write your answers, you may see a pattern form. You may find that your passion is closely tied to your personality preference. For instance, Popular Sanguines may be passionate in helping people to better their lives, Powerful Cholerics in raising funds for charity, Perfect Melancholies in doing research for terminal illnesses, or Peaceful Phlegmatics in mediating family conflicts.

Your passion will likely reflect your core values. Think of the beliefs that have significance and meaning to you, such as being helpful or courageous; having integrity and promoting justice, kindness, humility, laughter, respect, sportsmanship, etc. And don't forget: listen to your heart and keep your passion alive!

Your Turn

What do you value the most?

What stirs in your heart?

What excites you?

What intrigues you?

What breaks your heart?

What do you love doing?

Who do you love helping?

Review your responses, then translate them into a word or phrase that speaks to your heart. If you have difficulty figuring out your word or phrase, consider your top personal value or describe your favorite hobby.

I am most passionate about ______________________________.

Summary

Many people may have a dream unlived yet unforgotten. Meanwhile, others have a strong conviction to support a specific cause. This dream or conviction is a powerful motivator; it is a driving force that propels you to take action. It's time to rekindle this passion and build a plan to live your dream.

Let my heart be broken with the things that break the heart of God.
–Rev. Bob Pierce (1914–1978), founder of World Vision and Samaritan's Purse

Part Four

VISION AND CALLING

You will symbolically paint a picture of what success will look like in the next five, 10, or 20 years. This picture will serve as a blueprint for implementing that vision.

"Our calling is not primarily to be holy men and women,
but to be proclaimers of the gospel of God.
Personal holiness is an effect of redemption, not the cause of it."
–Oswald Chambers (1874–1917), writer, artist, musician

nine

VISUALIZE TO ACHIEVE

"'Even now,' declares the LORD,
'return to me with all your heart,
with fasting and weeping and mourning…
'And afterward,
I will pour out my Spirit on all people.
Your sons and daughters will prophesy,
your old men will dream dreams,
your young men will see visions…'"
–Joel 2:12, 28

"The imagination exercises a powerful influence over every act of sense, thought, reason, over every idea."
–Latin Proverb

AFTER READING *CHAPTER 3: AGING GRACEFULLY IN BODY, MIND, AND SPIRIT*, you've most likely made a commitment to exercising daily. Can you picture how you would look after three months of physical activity? I see myself like this: I am confidently sporting my short-sleeved purple polo T-shirt, without an oversized jacket to cover any belly fat. And there's no need for me to struggle as I smoothly zip up my size-28 fitted Buffalo blue jeans! Before, I used to grumble as I dragged myself to work out; now I appreciate my 20-minute brisk walks around the block. I envision myself being mentally fit, too: I am actively involved in something I cherish. My routine of reading, writing, preparing, and facilitating workshops invigorates me and I see myself learning something new each day.

What is your vision for the future? As you plan for the next stage of your life, creating your future reality in your mind will prompt you to take action. Past conversations with my high school friend Bernard have reminded me of the benefits and power of visioning. First, let me introduce you to Bernard, another baby boomer role model in terms of retiring early. Then I'll walk you through the key components of visioning.

Baby Boomer Role Model: Bernard

Bernard spent 25 years in the information technology scene, blending his work and family life into a hectic web. Bernard's average workweek alone was 80-plus hours. He lived through the dot-com era and witnessed the technology boom in Silicon Valley, on the West Coast of the United States, in the 2000s and retired just a couple of years ago—in his late 40s!

Sure, he had a successful career, but retiring early wasn't an easy decision for Bernard. However, his vision for the future motivated him to quit his job. He saw himself waking up every morning fully rested, savoring his morning coffee in his newly painted kitchen. Then he envisioned kissing his wife goodbye as she left for work. Next, Bernard drove his sons to school and picked them up from their badminton games and piano lessons. Every day, Bernard and his sons would laugh, chat, and enjoy each other's company. He also had a vision of visiting his elderly parents frequently, staying with them as long as he wanted to. Finally, he and his wife would make their way to China, to watch the beautiful sunset in the valley of Miyaluo, southwest of the Sichuan province.

As Bernard revealed his mental images to me, I noticed a sense of peace expressed on his face. His mental pictures of the future inspired him to say farewell to his frenzied work life. Now, he spends his retirement building closer relationships with his loved ones.

What's in a Vision?

When you project your thoughts into the future (thoughts which involve a highly desirable goal), you are creating an imminent reality, which impels you to live out that *imagined* reality. Thus, you can accomplish your goal. This is the power of visioning. You and I are capable of doing this with just a pen and a piece of paper to start. Let's review the three key components that encapsulate the visioning process:

1) Be specific
2) Be diligent
3) Be present

Be Specific

Initially, you can roughly describe what you want to see in your future. But you need to fill in the details. In the business world, we call this the future target state. The more specific you are, the more compelling your vision will be. I suggest you capture what you see or think on paper, or use the computer to type down your thoughts.

- **Step 1**: Write out a detailed description of what you want to accomplish.
- **Step 2:** Record your feelings that are attached to your intended accomplishment.

For example: Maybe you want to learn how to play the piano and you see yourself playing your favorite songs from the 70s. So you would write the following:

I look forward to my weekly piano lessons with Jill, my instructor. I enjoy my time with her because she pushes me to work on challenging pieces. I see myself sitting comfortably on the piano bench in my living room, practicing my scales every day. For years, I envied those who could read music and play the piano. Now, being able to play the entire *Let it Be* brings delight to my heart. I love it!

Be Diligent

Now that you see and feel what you want to accomplish, you need to act on it. Otherwise, you're only daydreaming. Start brainstorming the steps you need to take to achieve that goal. Try an iterative process, which means you don't need to be 100 percent correct in capturing all the necessary steps. Draft a few action items, elaborate, then make revisions if necessary. You may even discover new information about yourself as you start this visioning process. Be open to changes and enjoy this planning process. The deeper you get into this exercise, the more you'll take ownership of it. When you feel you own this plan, you will be drawn to making it happen.

***For example*:** You are a financial expert and you feel that today's youth lack money-management skills. You want to teach them how to avoid money pitfalls. So here's your vision:

You are touched to hear comments from the seminar participants who appreciate your willingness to share your wisdom. They feel their needs are being cared for! They see you as a loving mentor who exhibits Godly character! They find the seminar practical and they can apply the skills you have taught them right away. You also feel the excitement from the parents of these young people. They are relieved that their children will be spared from the misery of money issues.

After having this vision, you would take these actions:

1. Borrow some library books that show you how to create effective lesson plans.
2. Contact your church pastor and share your desire to start a new Sunday school series on financial management.

3. Arrange for an assistant to create promotional material for the upcoming seminar.
4. Organize your seminar materials.

Be Present

In this visioning process, imagine yourself actually living out your vision, reaping the benefits of your effort. When you start weaving your thoughts into the future you've painted for yourself (or the target state you have described), you will feel the joy of that outcome. You are motivated to continue supporting that vision because you are already living it mentally.

***For example*:** Consider my own experience as a worship leader who leads singing at church. One time, as I prepared to lead a song session, I imagined what I wanted to see: the congregation immersed in the experience rather than being spectators, passive participants or just going through the motions. As I was selecting songs for that Sunday, I started my visioning process: the brothers and sisters of my church appeared vividly in my mind as though I were standing in the sanctuary, leading worship singing. First, I was touched by my worship team's enthusiasm: four talented musicians on drums, guitar, keyboard, and bass were playing the songs skillfully, with a deep sense of offering their best to God. Then I saw the congregation singing along, joyfully following the rhythm with clapping hands. We were joining in one heart as we recited scriptures and prayed together. The whole sanctuary was filled with the sweet aroma of praise and worship. In my prayer, I prayed specifically for the worship team, asking God to touch them with the passion to serve Him fervently. I then prayed for the congregation for a renewed desire to draw close to God through corporate worship. That Sunday, the worship service was memorable. I felt an awesome presence of the Holy Spirit and the church had a wonderful encounter with God.

Visioning is powerful and inspiring, and creates hope. Have you lost hope in an unlived dream? Are there longings in your heart that you have long suppressed because you no longer believe they'll happen? Hopes and dreams for the future are powerful drivers for us to break new grounds. I want to assure you that God has a special plan for your life. I encourage you to see yourself as what God intended you to be. Believe in your potential and visualize what you are about to become.

Seeing Results Before They Happen

I have always dreamed about the future, even before I became a Christian. When I was young, my childhood fantasy was to be a movie star. I would sit in the corner of my family's small apartment, memorizing and rehearsing lines from a black-and-white movie. When my mother was nearby, I would recite those lines, animatedly pointing at her as though I were the main character in the movie *The Lost Princess' Adventure*.

As I blossomed into a teenager, my dream role shifted from movie star to pop star. I even learned to play the guitar and sing *Big Yellow Taxi*, just like Joni Mitchell. When no one was watching, I would even perform in front of the mirror wearing a pair of flared linen pants and red platform high heels. Though I still love acting and singing, those dreams never materialized. Over the years, I developed other interests such as teaching, writing, and public speaking. I later dreamed of becoming a motivational speaker, to share my life lessons with audiences around the world.

One thing all my dreams have in common is that they involve taking a platform or being on stage, sharing something with an audience, be it a skit, song, or message of some sort. After I had the conviction of living a life with purpose, I asked myself this simple question: why do I want to speak? Is it to satisfy my desire of becoming a star? Or is there something much deeper than mere self-promotion? I am convinced of the latter. I want to impact lives by sharing what God taught me through the years. In fact, each time I prepare for a speaking engagement or workshop, I usually complete a visioning exercise. I start by drafting a topic of interest, a short catch phrase that describes the subject of the talk. Then, I jot down a few points about my desired outcome. I elaborate on those key messages and enrich the points with stories and testimonies.

For instance, I recently spoke to a women's group about "Cultivating Harmony in Christian Marriages." To prepare for the content, I asked the meeting planner to tell me something about the target audience: their cultural background, age, professions, etc. I then asked myself what I wanted to see in these women after spending three hours in my conference. Next, I prayed to God, asking Him for the wisdom to address the needs of this congregation. I prayed for their faith to be strengthened and to apply more love and forgiveness in their relationships. Lastly, I pleaded to God to bring healing and restoration in broken relationships among those in need.

So, back to the original question: what did I want to see in these women after our time together?

Images of women hugging and encouraging each other came to mind. I also saw some of them sitting quietly, nodding with sincere smiles. I wanted to see three outcomes in particular:

1) *Commitment:* they will commit to becoming mature Christians by studying God's word and applying this knowledge into building harmony in their marriage.
2) *Better appreciation for individual differences:* they will improve their appreciation of their spouses, as they will understand the four primary personalities and the different life gifts. They will understand how God made each of us unique and that individual differences are healthy in a marriage for complementing strengths and weaknesses.
3) *Sacrificial love:* they will know the meaning of sacrificial love and will be ready to embrace this knowledge in marriage. They are willing to focus on the needs of their spouses rather than solely serving their own needs.

Using these images, I built my speech based on key points, along with instructions, life examples, and Bible references. In my mind, I was already engaging with my audience before meeting them. I sensed their eagerness in receiving God's word. I recognized their worthiness and their potential in becoming more Christ-like. I was energized to deliver my message. And when I actually met them, I felt like I was meeting old friends. In short, visualization helped me to achieve the goal of giving an effective presentation, thereby addressing the needs of the audience.

Visioning in Project Management

The value of visioning also applies to project management, helping to rein in ideas and put things into focus. One time, when I worked on a project to update a company website, senior management gave the team six months to complete the work. The project team spent many hours defining the scope without coming to a conclusion. We contemplated a wide range of possibilities: cleaning up and rewriting page content, rebranding the overall look and feel, redesigning the page layout, changing to a modern content-management platform, restructuring the backend database, you name it. The six-month project soon turned into a multiphase, yearlong initiative, with budget estimates that prohibited further consideration. The project sponsor graciously painted a picture of what success would look like: "This project is to review and revise the content of our company website such that information is accurate, straightforward, easy to find and relevant to the reader, using existing hardware and software infrastructure." With that, we nailed down the scope, rolled up our sleeves and worked towards fulfilling that vision. The new website was launched successfully in six months. And no doubt, the team was proud to have met the project goal.

Visioning is Relative to Your Life

Now you see how visioning helps achieve personal and project goals. The same principle applies to life planning. Pay special attention to your hopes and dreams. Do you believe in your dreams? Are you ready to dream immeasurably for God?

> God gives us dreams a size too big so that we can grow in them.
> –Author unknown

My favorite book is *The Alchemist* by Paulo Coelho, an adventure about Santiago, a 17-year-old shepherd boy. Santiago, believing in a recurring dream, is determined to fulfill his personal legend, which is to find treasure at the foot of the Egyptian pyramids. He travels many miles from Spain and encounters love, danger, disappointments, opportunity, and disaster, learning about himself and others along the way. Santiago found the treasure at the end. Achieving our legend is possible and is worth all the effort.

Achieving our legend is possible and is worth all the effort.

Many of us are realistic; we know our strengths and, even more so, our limitations. Many times, fear of failure holds us back in attempting something daring or prevents us from charting unfamiliar territories. When we're looking into the future 10- or 20-plus years and trying to determine how to live out God's plan, we need faith and courage. Remember, when Jesus looked at a person, He did not focus on weaknesses. He always saw the person in terms of what he or she could become. He believes in our potential. A good example is from John 4, when Jesus met the Samaritan woman. He did not see her as a prostitute; He saw what she could become and treated her with dignity. In His mercy, He gave her the living water. I invite you to believe in your dreams and follow them—be specific, be diligent, and be present. The only preparation you need is this: let loose, let go, and let God's power flow through you.

If God is for us, who can be against us?
–Romans 8:31

Imagine Your Passion

If people can't see what God is doing, they stumble all over themselves; But when they attend to what he reveals, they are most blessed.
–Proverbs 29:18, MSG

> What if you were to do something you absolutely enjoy?

What if you were to do something you absolutely enjoy? In this mental image, you are living God's plan for your life. Imagine the sense of achievement you would experience. Picture the smiles on people benefiting from your wisdom, service, product, or assistance. You would earn additional respect from your family, colleagues, friends, or even strangers. Imagine how excited you would feel about fulfilling your dream, carrying out the activities you're most passionate about.

Visualization Examples

My colleagues have visualized themselves:
- Going to school to study a topic they've never had time to explore in the past
- Volunteering regularly in a nursing home, orphanage or hospital
- Visiting prison inmates
- Cooking meals for the infirmed
- Delivering meals to the sick, disabled, or elderly
- Directing, managing, or supervising a team of youth workers
- Mentoring or coaching an individual entering the workforce

I encourage you to prayerfully reflect on your past experiences. Recall words of encouragement and affirmation, and suggestions people might have given you in the past; they could be from your boss, spouse, parents, teachers, colleagues, or your pastor. Listen carefully to the Holy Spirit's small voice.

You can start by thinking about what you're most passionate about. Is it cooking or teaching, singing or gardening, accounting or engineering? Then, think of how you can turn your passion into a solution that would make a difference in this world. For example, if you're like my girlfriend Connie, who adores traveling, you could consider combining your passion with evangelism in other countries. Connie doesn't see herself as a full-time missionary, but she does imagine sharing the gospel with someone during her travels. She can picture herself visiting orphanages in Africa, holding the hands of small children, hugging them, and reading Bible stories to them. She sees the children's innocent grins as she recalls Jesus' words:

> *Let the little children come to me, and do not hinder them, for the kingdom of God belongs to such as these.*
> –Luke 18:16

It's your turn to reflect on the following questions. Depending on where you are in your life journey, visioning may or may not be a familiar exercise for you. I encourage you to pause and consider what you see yourself doing or how you see yourself living in the near future. I invite you to take wild guesses, to keep your mind open. Be prepared to elaborate your 'yes' or 'no' responses.

1. What vision comes to mind after reading this chapter?

2. Is your vision propelling you to learn, explore, stretch, and grow? Explain your reason.

3. Is your vision propelling you to give, support, encourage, and transform others? Describe how your vision drives you to impact others.

4. Can you see how your vision is essential to your success in living out God's purpose in your life? If yes or no, how so?

5. Do you see yourself involved in a particular activity? Describe what you see.

6. What is your vision inspiring you to do?

7. Describe your environment, your surroundings. Who are you interacting with?

VISION POWER

Having a vision is powerful. Visualizing the outcome you want drives you to focus on making it a reality. In the next section, you will capture your vision of the future years with elation, blasting off like a cracking firework.

Visualizing the outcome you want drives you to focus on making it a reality.

After this, the word of the LORD came to Abram in a vision: "Do not be afraid, Abram. I am your shield, your very great reward."
–Genesis 15:1

SEEING BEYOND TODAY

Imagination is more important than knowledge.
–Albert Einstein (1879–1955), physicist, Nobel Prize recipient

You have grasped the power of visualization, thus contributing to your personal goal attainment and project success. Visualizing life at its fullest is the starting point for your retirement action plan.

If you're ready to take your zeal to the next level, focus on this chapter using your wildest imagination. Think of yourself as an architect; you are going to design the apogee, the pinnacle, the summit of your life, as if you're taking a ski lift up to the mountain top. You are going to create a conceptual view that captures your vision. (In the next chapter, you will take this conceptual view and develop a word picture that describes your vision in a succinct statement.)

Think of yourself as an architect; you are going to design the apogee, the pinnacle, the summit of your life, as if you're taking a ski lift up to the mountain top.

How to Break Down Your Vision

You've probably seen a sales brochure of a new housing construction project. Usually on the first page, you'll see a very grandiose and enticing picture; this is an artist's conceptual view of the new subdivision. You see rows of trees planted beside a well-landscaped pond, young families strolling leisurely alongside the pond with their small children, and teenagers riding their bikes around the neighborhood or gathering around, chatting heartily. The houses are laid out on both sides of the crescent, designed with natural stones, brick columns, and tall windows. It is surely a beautiful view, yet it is only the artistic concept. In reality, the piece of land is still not developed. Drive by the site and you will see a huge piece of dormant farmland.

In the upcoming exercise, you are the lead artist or chief architect responsible for visualizing a conceptual view of your retirement. First, pay special attention to the physical environment; secondly, the people involved; and lastly, place yourself in this view.

I've asked you this question already, but I am going to ask you again: what would happen if you were to do something you absolutely enjoy? This thought is stimulating, invigorating, and unstoppable. The key is to visualize your dream retirement as though it has already come true, just like flipping through the housing sales brochure. Painting a mental picture will help break your dream down to the physical environment and the people who would be impacted by your actions. In this section, I've created a hands-on worksheet to help you visualize your retirement. I will ask a question, show you an example, and then you will have your turn to pause, reflect, and fill in your answer.

Physical environment

- What is happening around you?

Example: If you enjoy arts and crafts, you may see yourself designing home decor. You're taking it beyond a hobby; you are helping your friends to re-decorate their homes with new curtains and cushions.

Your Turn:

- Where are your actions taking place?

Example: You're browsing a fabric store, choosing materials for your project.

Your Turn:

- What stands out in your surroundings? (Note: consider what you see, how the people around you react, what they think of you, etc.)

Example: The latest styles and colors of fabric, lace, and trims are fascinating. You can't wait to get your hands on the new velvety, earth-tone designs. Your friends are so proud when they receive your finished products and they're thrilled at the sight of their living room makeover! They enjoy the new curtains and cushions so much, they can't thank you enough.

Your Turn:

The People

- Who is encouraging you to excel?

Example: Your daughters think you are a sewing genius and they want you to make their wedding dresses. Your friends are amazed at your creativity; they want you to teach them how to sew. They also refer their friends to talk to you about decorating their homes.

Your Turn:

- Who is benefitting from your actions?

Example: Your daughters, your family, your friends, their families, etc.

Your Turn:

Yourself

- How do you look? (Note: consider your facial expressions, attire, energy level, mood, etc.)

Example: I am diligent, happy, and energetic. I am wearing my casual, comfortable sweatshirt and sweatpants, busily working away on my sewing project—placing silvery trims along the curtain hems.

Your Turn:

- How do you feel?

Example: I feel satisfied, fulfilled, and productive. I am glad my hobby can brighten lives.

Your Turn:

- Describe your spiritual connection with Jesus.

Example: When I look at the beautiful cushions, curtains, beddings, etc., I realize that God is the greatest artist of all. He knitted us uniquely as individuals. We are all made from different fabrics with kaleidoscopic designs. Each type of fabric is valuable material for a different purpose. For example, a piece of white cotton fabric is useful for making a washable tablecloth. A piece of colorful silk is handy for a scarf. A piece of sturdy denim is practical for a pair of jeans. Discovering who I am is like discovering the underlying fabric of my life. Living out God's plan in my life is to make the best use of the fabric, becoming the handiwork that glorifies the master designer—our Maker.

Your Turn:

Marking Mental Milestones

After answering the questions, the next step is to break down your vision into milestones. A milestone can be considered as a major landmark or significant event. (For instance, a 10-year wedding anniversary is a milestone.) These milestones are helpful for designing a progression of achievements or tangible results rather than taking one big leap. Milestones are especially advantageous when learning a new skill or planning an activity with different phases. If you've always enjoyed music, for example, but you've never had a chance to take piano lessons, your retirement offers an opportunity for you to take weekly lessons. So maybe your plan is to complete a Grade 5 Royal Conservatory Certificate in five years' time; thus, setting a milestone to mark that achievement will give you a target to work towards. On the other hand, if you want to devise finer milestones (such as making a one-year mark), you can do that, too.

Here's your chance to reflect on your retirement milestones. Using similar techniques that you have mastered from the visioning exercises above, imagine yourself already retired and answer these questions:

What does your retirement look like in the next five years?

What does your retirement look like in the next 10 years?

What does your retirement look like in the next 20 years?

Summary

Visualizing life at its fullest is the starting point for your retirement action plan. You have pictured and understood your retirement according to God's plan for your life. Prepare to grasp God's richness and live each day to its fullest. God is the one who reveals what His people need. I pray that you may catch on to His revelation and be obedient in carrying out the work. In the next chapter, you will put together a word picture that describes God's calling for your retirement.

So we fix our eyes not on what is seen, but on what is unseen, since what is seen is temporary, but what is unseen is eternal.
–2 Corinthians 4:18

When we strive to become better than we are, everything around us becomes better, too.
–Paulo Coelho, best-selling author

ten

WHAT IS YOUR CALLING?

"For it is by grace you have been saved, through faith—and this not from yourselves, it is the gift of God—not by works, so that no one can boast. For we are God's handiwork, created in Christ Jesus to do good works, which God prepared in advance for us to do."
–Ephesians 2:8–10

"The tragedy of life is what dies inside a man while he lives."
–Albert Schweitzer (1875–1965), German medical missionary, theologian, and musician

"Anybody can do anything that he imagines."
–Henry Ford, founder of Ford Motor Company

IN 2004, I PURCHASED SIX COPIES OF THE SAME BOOK FOR MY WHOLE family. I believed the book was so significant, that everyone—including my nine-year-old son, Isaac—needed to study and follow the principles it discussed. This is what I wrote on the inside cover of Isaac's copy of the *Purpose Driven Life* by Rick Warren:

Dear Isaac,
You're very special! The Almighty God revealed Himself to you when you were very young so that you will walk in His path. He will keep you from stumbling to the many temptations on this earth. May the Holy Spirit guide you to fully explore the purpose for your life. To Him be the glory!
Amen,
Mom

Needless to say, writing out this prayer was a defining life moment. I have been acting on it ever since. My belief in God, my relationship with Jesus Christ, my struggles in balancing work, family, and ambition started falling into place, fitting into a bigger picture. But the picture resembled the back of a framed tapestry: I could see a mumble-jumble of threads in random colors, tangled, patched, frayed and intermittently knotted.

In my mind, something significant was going to happen. I was anticipating a drastic change, a big bang, a radical revelation or something that had a profound impact on what I was doing—it would also have a long-lasting effect on the rest of my life. Surely enough, the anticipation came alive as a vigorous mental exercise, which paved a path for discovering my life mission.

What is a Mission?

The *Canadian Oxford Dictionary* defines mission as "a particular task or goal assigned to a person or group." This meaning suggests that there is a caller to assign the task or goal to a person or group. The person or group who responds to this task or goal takes on a journey with a special purpose in mind. Therefore, mission may be considered a religious concept that involves the caller and a responder. The caller determines the destiny for those who are being called upon. The caller is the sovereign God, the Creator of this universe who determined the destination for each of us. Therefore, the people being called—you and me—can't possibly create that sense of purpose. This mission needs to be revealed by the caller and it needs to be discovered by you and me.

> This mission needs to be revealed by the caller and it needs to be discovered by you and me.

Understanding the concept of mission is foundational in helping us appreciate God's two-level plan for His people. It involves the Great Commission for the human race (which I will discuss momentarily) and a personal calling. The Bible provides the assurance that God is actively guiding us to carry out our lifelong service into retirement.

During the history of the lives of the Israelites—when they were kept in captivity in Babylon (as recorded in the Old Testament)—through the words of the prophet Jeremiah, God spoke of His plans for His beloved children and His willingness to guide them to prosperity:

> *This is what the LORD says: "When 70 years are completed for Babylon, I will come to you and fulfill my good promise to bring you back to this place. For I know the plans I have for you," declares the LORD, "plans to prosper you and not to harm you, plans to give you hope and a future. Then you will call on me and come and pray to me, and I will listen to you. You will seek me and find me when you seek me with all your heart. I will be found by you," declares the LORD.*
> –Jeremiah 29:10–14

God has great plans for His people, plans that encourage optimism and hope into the future; plans that lead to victory instead of impairment. God also promises His presence with those who earnestly pursue Him. However, His assurance from the above passage requires us to look beyond the current circumstances, to take courage in inventing the future by seeking out His plans faithfully. His plans for us can be perceived in two levels: macro and micro.

The Great Commission

On a macro level, God has designed a grand plan of salvation for the entire human race. Out of His love, He desires everyone to have eternal life. On a micro level, God has a plan that leads us to personal success and hope for the future. God sent Jesus Christ to this earth so that His grand plan of salvation and the individual (personal) plan could be accomplished. Jesus is the bridge that connects us to the Creator of this universe. Those who believe in Jesus as the Son of God who died for our sins will be given eternal life.

> *For God so loved the world that he gave his one and only Son, that whoever believes in him shall not perish but have eternal life.*
> –John 3:16

Jesus started His earthly ministry at the age of 30 and changed history in three short years. Though He faced rejection, His purpose on earth was clearly lived and God's plan was fully revealed. The accounts of Jesus were vividly recorded in the four Gospels. Despite the fact that Jesus performed miracles in healing the sick, casting out demons, and rendering teachings, He was mocked, scourged, and crucified by those who opposed Him. He was charged with the offense of blasphemy, claiming to be the Son of God. His accusers in the Roman Empire failed to recognize that He was the Messiah, the Christ and Savior sent by God to bring peace to mankind. Although Jesus died on the cross in agony, He conquered death and broke the chains of hell. On the third day, Jesus returned to earth briefly in His resurrected body, appearing to His disciples with a significant message:

> *Therefore go and make disciples of all nations, baptizing them in the name of the Father and of the Son and of the Holy Spirit and*

teaching them to obey everything I have commanded you. And surely I am with you always, to the very end of the age.
–Matthew 28:18–20

A commission is an instruction or command given to a person or group. Bible scholars labeled the last five verses in Matthew 28 as the *Great Commission*. This was Jesus' command to His followers. Here, Jesus provided clear instructions for His disciples, assuring them of His indefinite presence.

The directives Jesus gave the disciples are a culmination of what they experienced in their journey together. Jesus basically instructed the disciples to continue what He had done during His three years of earthly ministry. His disciples were instructed to:

a) Actively evangelize and influence everyone they met to emulate the way of life that Jesus demonstrated.
b) Confirm their commitment by baptism in the name of the Holy Trinity: Father, Son, and Holy Spirit, regardless of their nationality.
c) Provide training, mentoring, and support to those people baptized so that they will live according to the commandments given by Jesus.
d) Realize that Jesus' presence will be with them forever.

In Relation to Today

What does the Great Commission have to do with us today? The instructions were originally given to the 11 disciples Jesus appeared and spoke to. However, since Jesus commanded the 11 disciples to "go and make disciples of all nations," this implied that the number of disciples would be multiplied as they evangelized, converted, baptized, taught, and trained others. This becomes a perpetual call that involves all disciples or followers of Jesus Christ, including you and me.

When we take the challenge to witness the love and redemption of Jesus Christ, the grand plan of God's salvation can be accomplished.

We can be the agents of change in fulfilling God's macro-level plan. If each believer evangelizes and mentors one disciple every year, it will take less than 33 years to cover the world's population of seven billion, says Dr. Billie Hanks Jr., founder of the ministry *Operation Multiplication.*[57] Let's break it down: if one believer mentors a disciple each year, the number of disciples per year doubles. If we start with two people in the first year, there will be four disciples in the second year, eight in the third… and by the 20th year, there will be more than a million disciples. By the 30th year, there will be over a billion disciples. This good news can feasibly be preached to the entire human race within a lifetime.

Now let's use this math to focus on Christian baby boomers in Canada, the largest population of retirees and those soon to be retiring. There are over nine million baby boomers in Canada; assuming one in five is a Christian, we potentially have 1.8 million baby boomer evangelists ready to spread the good news to the ends of the earth. By the second year, there will be 3.6 million Christians. If each Christian continues to bring up one disciple every year, by the end of the 13th year, the entire world's population of seven billion would become disciples. Do you see yourself living to view this transformation? If you're 55 years old, you will be 68 by the time this happens. Are you excited to see the possibilities ahead?

Why Find Your Calling?

It is hard to imagine why people would refuse prosperity. However, we see many who wander aimlessly for the next thrill and they become disillusioned and wary. Or others lead busy lives yet they feel unfulfilled or unsure whether they're doing the right things for God.

God made it clear to the enslaved, exiled Israelites that He planned to give them hope and a bright future (Jeremiah 29:10–14). God's nature does not change through time. Those who actively respond by seeking Him with a sincere heart will find Him. He will direct their paths to prosperity as well. On the contrary, if we live without knowing our life calling, we are missing out on God's wonderful design, His vast resources and wisdom. Imagine walking through life with a pair of shady tinted sunglasses all day, only detecting dark images without appreciating the various vibrant colors, light, shades, and details which make life meaningful to you and others. Are you willing to settle for dark images rather than seeing all the colorful intricacies of your life picture?

Here are the benefits to discovering your life calling:

- Knowing one's calling in life cultivates a sense of mission.
- The sense of mission gives us a purpose to live.
- A purpose to live brings clarity to our ultimate life goal.
- This life goal forms a long-term target that provides a sense of direction, guiding our actions for the next day, month, or years.
- This sense of direction helps us focus our limited energy and resources on the right endeavors. It helps us to accept or decline invitations that deviate from our goals.
- This sense of direction propels us to move forward, especially when life gets tough.

Link Your Calling with Your Life Mission

Defining your life mission is a response to God's calling for your life. For a person who does not believe in a sovereign Creator in charge of the universal order, this mission can only be considered as one's life goal or purpose; it ends with one's physical existence. Also, there is no accountability to a higher authority. On the contrary, to someone who has a relationship with the Creator and believes God loves him or her immensely, the reason for living means more than the here and now. There is a special purpose to be fulfilled. The earthly journey is a preparation for a life that carries on beyond our imagination. It will be a life spent in eternity with Him, who orchestrated the placement of the stars, the sun, the moons, and the magnificent galaxies. In His infinite wisdom, He created us with eternity in mind.

He has made everything beautiful in its time. He has also set eternity in the human heart; yet no one can fathom what God has done from beginning to end.
–Ecclesiastes 3:11

The life mission concept takes on a much more profound significance; it not only provides the reason for our existence and purpose, it also gives us the tenacity for living and the hope for a glorious life to come. Finding and living out this purpose answers our call to the caller, God. We will be giving an account of our lives when we meet Him face to face in heaven. If we do not know our calling or special purpose on earth, it's like having lived in a house full of unopened gifts. Do we want to meet Him in heaven with an unlived life? Do you really want to put off finding out your calling for another year?

If we do not know our calling or special purpose on earth, it's like having lived in a house full of unopened gifts.

However, I consider my life worth nothing to me; my only aim is to finish the race and complete the task the Lord Jesus has given me—the task of testifying to the good news of God's grace.
–Acts 20:24

Recognize Your Calling

Many of us have lived close to or more than half a century, with loads of experience under our belts. Seniors have even more valuable life experiences. Or maybe you're still young, but want to make the most of your life ahead. Have all your ambitious aspirations turned into glowing accomplishments? Do you already have answers to the following questions?

- What do I want to be remembered for after my earthly journey is over?
- Why am I here on earth?
- There are many worthwhile causes that require extra help. Which one do I feel most compelled to spend my energy and resources on?
- The Bible states, "I am fearfully and wonderfully made." For what purpose, though?
- Why do I have a nagging dream that does not seem to go away?

If you already have the answers to the above questions, I sincerely congratulate you and encourage you to reflect on discovering your life purpose in the next section of this chapter. I hope you'll take this opportunity to seek further revelation from God as you review your impact on the world around you and ask Him to expand your territory of influence moving forward. If you do not already have answers to the questions, I prayerfully invite you to follow the next section. You will unfold the most exciting message about yourself that will lead you to new wonders in your remaining years.

> Life can only be understood backwards; but it must be lived forwards.
> –Soren Kierkegaard (1813–1855), Danish philosopher, theologian, and religious author

Journey of Discovery

In November 2004, as my church wrapped up the *Forty Days of Purpose Campaign* based on Rick Warren's *Purpose Driven Life*, our senior pastor, Rev. Sit, challenged the congregation to act upon our life purpose. The sermon title, *Defining My Life Mission,* captivated my attention. I frantically took notes as Rev. Sit presented the details in his 40-minute sermon; after all, my New Year's resolution for 2005 was to complete my own mission statement. Boy, was it much harder than I expected! This was more than just a writing assignment; rather, it was an eye-opening, invigorating, and life-changing journey that drew my relationship closer to our Creator. I was about to re-engineer what I thought God wanted me to do with my life.

After many late nights of self-questioning, meditating, reminiscing, reading, researching, and contemplating my purpose, I visualized success for my project management consulting business. Here was what I saw:

> I have clients who value my expertise in my service. We are mutually engaged in achieving organizational goals. My clients come exclusively through referrals, allowing me to spend less time in marketing and to devote my energy in planning and delivering my service. I am organized, dependable, client-focused, efficient, and well-liked. My clients are ethical and committed to excellence. They pay me above industry standards and they are on time with their payments. I build long-term relationships with the people I serve and they are interested in my well-being, as they are their own.

That was as far as I could go at the time. It was a good exercise, because it helped me visualize my characteristics and the quality of my service. However, did God place me in this world to glorify Him through good work in project management? He must have, for this is what I have been doing quite successfully for the past decade. But my purpose is more than being an extraordinary consultant or having satisfied clients. How does the work of a project management consultant relate to accomplishing the Great Commission, which is to make disciples of all nations? So, I spent more time and money on books, researching topics on self-discovery, mission, and purpose. I started to understand how God prepared me to act on my passion by utilizing life gifts, abilities, my personality, and experiences gained through my different roles: mother, teacher, consultant, project manager, counselor, and such. I learned the following principles about a life mission:[58]

a) *A life mission is bigger than a goal.* Getting clients to pay me on time is a goal, but it is not a life purpose. People can set many goals, but achieving them all does not make up a life mission.

b) *A life mission is more than a reflection of your role.* We play many roles in the different stages of life. My role as a mother will no longer be a primary focus when my children are grown. Likewise, I may change jobs or professions over the course of my career. I may also retire from an active working life.

c) *A life mission reflects the values you believe are most important to God.* God's value system is quite different than what the world thinks is important. God loves us all and He desires for no one to perish; instead, individuals shall have eternal life through believing in Him and accepting Jesus Christ as their personal Savior.

d) *A life mission describes what you were made to do through discovery and revelation.* My life mission is an expression of God's purpose for my life. Defining my life mission involves self-discovery and a divine revelation from God. It does not come automatically.

e) *A life mission expresses my passion, values, life gifts, abilities, personality, and experiences.* God is purposeful; He holds us accountable for the resources that He entrusts us with (see Matthew 25:14–30, the parable of the talents). God has given us certain interests, talents, and backgrounds to help fulfill our life missions.

Using the above principles, I refined my earlier drafted vision. By the end of 2006, I had put together a statement that describes what I believe God wants me to do with my life. This simple sentence formed the guideposts for my later years. As I read it today, it still reflects and affirms what I'm striving for. Finally, the framed tapestry had revealed itself more clearly—it was no longer a mishmash of threads.

Today, the tapestry is a piece of magnificent art with rich, vibrant colors, meticulously textured with stunning patterns. The detailed arrays continue, though; the tapestry is not complete, but the finished handiwork will be magnificent and flawless. This is the nature of our God, the one who is weaving the fabric of our lives.

My revised vision for the future takes on a much broader and holistic view, and it looks like this:

I see my family, friends, clients, and workshop participants fulfilling their life purpose and enjoying their well-being. They are:

- Growing in spiritual maturity
- Leading balanced lives in body, mind, and spirit
- Enjoying meaningful relationships
- Engaging in activities that they are most passionate about
- Resilient and able to bounce back when faced with pain, suffering, challenges, setbacks, and discouragements
- Free from undue worries
- Feeling fulfilled and hopeful about the future

Seeing others live out their potential, grow in their faith, stand firm in the midst of trials, and have a positive outlook brings joy to my heart. I feel excited waking up every morning with the prospect of enriching others. I have a part to play in bringing this vision to fruition. My role is to be an encourager, a teacher, a workshop facilitator, a motivational speaker, and a friend, to bring about positive change in someone's life. This is my calling. As a statement, it reads like this:

My mission is to inspire, equip, and mobilize people to live life to its fullest.

You have just reviewed an example of my own journey in defining my mission statement, which captures my life calling. In Chapter 11, I will discuss how to craft specific and realistic objectives, which have helped me achieve my mission.

EXAMPLES OF LIFE MISSION STATEMENTS BY OTHER MIDDLE-AGERS

"My mission in life is to learn to live a good and faithful life in order to lead others to live a good and faithful life."
–Clement Shim, civil engineer, part-time seminary student

"My mission is to build positive and healthy communities and to be an influence in transforming individuals to express God's love."
–Gus Liam, social worker

"It is my mission to influence all those with whom my life intersects, to become all that God intends them to be."
–David Lewis, pastor and leadership coach

"The purpose of my life is to humbly serve our Lord by being a… passionate example of the absolute joy that is available to us the moment that we rejoice in God's gifts…"
–Anthony Robbins, author and motivational speaker

The discipline of writing something down is the first step toward making it happen.
–Lee Iacocca, former president of Ford, founder of the Lacocca Foundation

The Art and Science of a Life Mission Statement

Where is the starting point for defining your life mission? In the previous chapter, we discussed the power of having a vision, as it helps us envisage something great before it happens. It provides a mental blueprint for us to move forward in achieving an action. Defining your life mission starts with a mental picture of what you think God calls you to do, which will advance the Great Commission (of making disciples of all nations), determine who you will impact, and the changes that occur as a result of such impact.

You can create your own success story; first, visualize what you want success to look like. Here is the formula for capturing that:

Do What* + *To Whom* + *So What

Do What: *What do you think God calls you to do for advancing the Great Commission?*

Think about a particular interest you are most passionate about, an area you're drawn to making a difference in. It may be general or broad such as physical, mental, or spiritual health, beauty, art, social justice, entertainment, science, environment, sustainability, food, nutrition, finance, etc. Or, it may be a specific area in which you're gifted. Also think about your talents and abilities that people value or appreciate the most.

To Whom: *Who is your target audience? Who do you want to serve? Or which groups of people appeal to you the most?*

Consider those you relate to best (young children, adolescents, teens, career-minded adults, middle-aged adults, married couples, divorced individuals, single parents, the elderly, orphans, prisoners, abuse victims, those with special needs, etc.) For example, you may be passionate in supporting the needs of single mothers; then your target organization to serve could be local shelters for single moms or abused women.

***So What**: What are the results of such an impact?*

Think about how your actions can change people's lives. For example, if you are passionate in teaching financial management to teenagers, what is the result of educating them? They would avoid financial pitfalls that others wouldn't know how to avoid. And there is the indirect impact that should not be overlooked. As a result of having good financial management skills, these teenagers will grow up and coach their children to manage money. Overall, your result can be general and broad or specific and focused.

- *General and Broad Result*

  You may impact your target group in a way that strengthens one or more aspects of the spiritual fruit: love, joy, peace, patience, kindness, goodness, faithfulness, gentleness, or self-control. This is the outcome of a changed life through the power of the Holy Spirit. Or the impact may involve the improved well-being of the body, mind, and/or spirit. Consider how you can influence lives in each dimension.

- *Specific and Focused Result*

  You may impact your target group by helping them solve a problem, thus addressing a specific need. If you're a carpenter, the result of your actions could be as specific as this: you benefit people by making good-quality furniture that enriches their living environment. Or as a dance teacher, you promote your students' interest in the art and train them to become professional performers.

Let's take this formula and work on your life mission. Writing down your thoughts will encourage you to focus on your objectives, remember ideas, and reach your goals. (You can refer to the samples in each section to help create your own statement.) The purpose of the word-bank is to provide you with word choices; you can pick a word from the lists or use words that aren't listed. There are no wrong answers. If you find it difficult to capture your words, pray to

God for patience and His revelation. Use the process of elimination and keep searching.

Do What

Write what you think God calls you to do for advancing the Great Commission.

Samples:

God calls me to encourage and affirm through teaching.

Or

My mission in life is to empower and instruct those who are hurt and discouraged.

Your Turn:

God calls me to ________________________________

Or

My mission in life is to ____________________________

DO WHAT—ACTION WORD-BANK

Accomplish	Achieve	Advance	Affirm	Alleviate	Amplify
Brighten	Build	Compel	Communicate	Complete	Compose
Confirm	Connect	Create	Cultivate	Defend	Deliver
Demonstrate	Direct	Discover	Educate	Edify	Embrace
Encourage	Enlighten	Excite	Explore	Facilitate	Foster
Gather	Generate	Give	Grow	Implement	Improve
Inform	Influence	Inspire	Instruct	Introduce	Involve
Launch	Lead	Mediate	Mitigate	Model	Motivate
Nurture	Open	Organize	Participate	Perform	Praise
Present	Prepare	Produce	Promote	Preserve	Provide
Pursue	Reclaim	Reflect	Reform	Revise	Re-establish
Sacrifice	Safeguard	Save	Serve	Share	Speak
Stand	Support	Surrender	Sustain	Take charge	Travel
Teach	Touch	Understand	Unify	Use	Validate
Validate	Volunteer	Work	Win	Write	Yield

To Whom

Write down who your target audience is. Who do you want to serve? Or which groups of people appeal to you the most?

Samples:

I relate best to teenagers.

Or

I am most effective working with educated young professionals.

Or

I am most passionate when helping abused women.

Your Turn:

I relate best to ______________________________

Or

I am most effective when working with __________________

Or

I am most passionate when helping _____________________

TO WHOM—TARGET GROUP WORD-BANK

Population by Demographic	Special Need or Interest Groups	Groups by Profession
Unborn infants	The homeless	Teachers
Babies	Children with disabilities	Social workers
Toddlers	Adults with disabilities	Engineers
Children	Families with disabled children	Clergy
Pre-teens	Blended families	Police
Teens	Divorced families	Techies
Adolescents	Single parents	Healthcare professionals
College/University students	Widows	Tradesmen
Career-minded adults	Abuse victims	Hospitality workers
Young couples	Gifted children	Business owners
The middle-aged	Substance abusers/addicts	Government officials
The empty nesters	Orphans	Politicians
The baby boomers	Veterans	Artists
The elderly	The unemployed	Musicians
The retirees	People in career transition	Marketers

So What

Write down the results of such impact.

Samples:

As a result of my encouragement and affirmation, my students will become more confident in themselves.

Or

As a result of my teaching and coaching, my students will secure respectable jobs and maintain a decent living.

Or

As a result of my mentoring, my students will write an award-winning book or article.

Or

My client will learn effective ways to cope with her loss and get out of the current depressed state through the counseling process.

Your Turn:

(Note: Remember, your results can be broad or general, specific or focused.)

As a result of my ________________________________

Or

My clients will __________________________________

Your next job is to formulate one sentence (preferably) or a couple of sentences by reviewing your answers in the *Do What, To Whom,* and *So What* sections. It's not important to use every word from those sections. Read them through a few times to understand the essence that draws you in. You may find it helpful to use scrap paper to jot down a basic sentence for expansion or to trim down unnecessary phrases. (Some people prefer to use a computer to type out a rough draft of their life mission statement.) The following examples give you some ideas to start. Feel free to cut and paste phrases for your own draft.

My life mission is to:

Encourage teenagers by affirming their self-worth as children of God.

Bring hope to those who are being neglected by society so that they can develop life skills, enabling them to become the best they can be.

Evangelize teenagers and encourage them to experience God by building a regular devotional life.

Equip teenagers to develop exceptional financial management skills so they'll be faithful stewards when they grow up.

Lead others to offer worship to God by singing beautiful praise songs.

Evangelize to children and equip them to be worshippers so that they will not depart from their faith when they grow up.

Fill in your life mission below:

____

TIME FOR YOU TO SHINE

The Bible is a reminder of God's immense love for us and that He has a purpose. He will not withhold any goodness from us; people who have trusted this promise and experienced God in a personal way will testify this truth. Meditate on these words and capture your thoughts with the following passages:

And I pray that you, being rooted and established in love, may have power, together with all the Lord's holy people, to grasp how wide and long and high and deep is the love of Christ, and

to know this love that surpasses knowledge—that you may be filled to the measure of all the fullness of God.
–Ephesians 3:17–19

...for it is God who works in you to will and to act in order to fulfill his good purpose.
–Philippians 2:13

Summary

Knowing your life calling helps validate your vision and provides a rationale to why you should be doing certain actions. When we're living life to its fullest, we're able to exercise our talents, gifts, skills, and experience in a way that only we can deliver. By now, you have gained better clarity to the why, what, where, and who you are meant to serve.

The Mighty One, God, the LORD, speaks and summons the earth from the rising of the sun to where it sets. From Zion, perfect in beauty, God shines forth.
–Psalm 50:1–2

The next part of this book will guide you to put your plan together for short-, medium-, and long-term actions. This will not be a one-time exercise. Planning includes continuous evaluations of what works, what doesn't, and how to improve our actions. As organizational effectiveness requires continuous improvement, so does living a purposeful life.

Life is a precious gift and I don't intend to waste a day of it.
–Jai Pausch, author of *Dream New Dreams*

Part Five

PUT LEGS TO YOUR PLAN

Plan your work and work your plan. In this final part of the book, you'll use tools to develop a measurable action plan. This will help you reimagine yourself, in turn guiding you to commendably arrive at your destination. You'll be able to focus your time on the aspects that are aligned with your calling.

"Action without vision is a nightmare.
Vision without action is a daydream."
–Japanese Proverb

eleven

THE THREE STEPS TO SUCCESS

"Ask and it will be given to you; seek and you will find; knock and the door will be opened to you."
–Matthew 7:7

"What is now proved was once imagined."
–William Blake (1757–1827), English poet

OSWALD CHAMBERS ONCE NOTED HOW WE PRIMARILY SUBMIT OUR spiritual issues to God. But when it comes to daily issues, we don't necessarily put Him first. Perhaps it's because we're trained to be independent thinkers, doers, and problem-solvers. When we're stuck in traffic, we likely reach for the GPS to find alternative routes, rather than seek God's intervention to relieve the congestion. Can we look to the same God who parted the Red Sea to make a dry path for the Israelites over two thousand years ago to fix our traffic jams?

SAME GOD, DIFFERENT ERA

Psalm 102:25–27 speaks of the unchanging, perfect nature of God. Heaven and earth will perish, but He will remain the same.

God is interested in the whole person, including his or her daily living. Chambers reminded us to put Him first in all aspccts of our lives—that includes planning for the future.

> *In the beginning you laid the foundations of the earth, and the heavens are the work of your hands. They will perish, but you remain; they will all wear out like a garment…*
> *But you remain the same, and your years will never end.*
> –Psalm 102:25–27

We've already seen how God blesses His people—even unto old age—in the previous chapters of this book. He is faithful in guiding us as we plan our journey forward. God is depicted as a kind, earthly parent who gives his son the best gifts. If the son asks for bread, he will not respond by giving him a stone. I challenge you to make bold requests to God, for He cares for your well-being. He wants to see us happy, content, and fulfilled. He wants us to explore all that life has to offer, to finish well on this earthly voyage before returning to our eternal home—where we will meet Him face to face.

Knock and Wait

Aligning your ambition with God's plan is necessary before asking Him to fulfill requests. This is in line with Jesus' teaching to first seek the kingdom of God and His righteousness (Matthew 6:33).

Therefore, we need to understand that not everything we ask for shall be given to us. We are to submit to God's sovereign will and His timing. Rejoicing when the doors open for us seems like a no-brainer. We surely remember the time we won against tough competition for a job posting, earned the employee of the month award, or attained the gold medal at the marathon. What about facing closed doors that deny your entry into a dream job? Receiving heartbreaking news about a critical illness? Do you still see the footprints of God carrying you through a different door? When you need to scale-down your dreams due to life circumstances, stand firm in faith. I pray that you experience a sense of joy, comfort, and peace during both triumph and adversity.

We don't all experience smooth sailing throughout our lives. Life can challenge us beyond what we think we're capable of handling. Submitting to God's will and searching and discovering our life calling can transform what feels like a broken life into one that is gratifying and even joyful. My mentor nods her head with an assuring smile and stretches both arms to soothe her achy back as she shares her story. Here's her bittersweet condensed memoir.

Mary Lou's Story

"This is not what I hoped for," Mary Lou protests. As she enters her senior years, she finds that the plans she had for retirement, made as a young woman, are unlikely to be fulfilled. "I was drawn to a fast-paced life where getting things done, writing exhilarating screenplays, travelling and exploring exotic places of the world were essential for my well-being." She speaks with intensity as she shares her aspirations.

Mary Lou worked hard to shape her personal legend during her early 20s. She studied journalism at university, built a portfolio of screenplays, and managed to win the support from a prominent agent to help launch her career in screenwriting in Hollywood. This was her best-laid plan, dream, and life-script.

Mary Lou never made it to Hollywood. Instead of making her mark in the entertainment industry, her life was scarred with pain, loss, hurt, grief, and disappointment. A car accident completely altered her own life-script in her 30s. Mary Lou became disabled, lost her physical stamina, and was left with body-wide chronic pain. For many years, Mary Lou wrestled with God and pleaded for nothing else except to be free of pain and able to do what other healthy people did. She prayed for divine healing.

Though Jesus healed lepers by his touch, Jesus did not answer Mary Lou the same way. Pain and fatigue remained; dreams and ambitions vanished and yet, miraculously, Mary Lou gained a renewed hope. Now in her 50s, she feels content and peaceful. Overwhelmed by God's saving grace, she recognizes her self-centeredness and imperfections. Her spiritual strength overtakes her physical limitation and financial uncertainty.

Can a person who struggles with lingering pain and lives on a small, limited income experience joy and live her life calling? Mary Lou responded in an astounding "yes." Writing for children is now Mary Lou's passion. While she can only work for about an hour a day at it, that hour, she says, is precious. She hopes someday to see her stories in print and that the spiritual truths within them will impact young lives. Mary Lou chooses to store her riches in heaven as she engages in life-long service to mentor others. Mary Lou exercises her gifts and talents in journalism by mentoring other writers like me through critiques and editing.

Now, Mary Lou is living an abundant life, continuing to fulfill her new dream while awaiting the triumphant call to eternity.

Hopeful Anticipation

Success is beyond the achievements you have already coveted. When we take inventory of our gifts, talents, and interests, a heavenly standard—rather than a worldly one—should measure our goals in life. When we attempt things that stretch beyond our abilities, or when we reshape our dreams due to life circumstances, it would humble us to seek God's will.

Living life to its full potential is a continual process—until we are called home. Finishing well on this earthly journey does not mean claiming a one-time prize. It's a perpetual measure that we strive for since we never know when our end point will happen. For some, this desirable outcome may happen within a year or two. For others, it could be 30 years.

Living life to its full potential is a continual process—until we are called home.

The Three-Step Strategy

As you pray for God's guidance, use the three-step strategy to put your plan into action. The three-step strategy, as illustrated in the diagram below, is a repetitive approach that requires you to reflect, imagine, and reinvent your future endeavors. Reflect on what matters to you the most (your successes, failures, and lessons learned). Imagine a new state of being, a different outcome, or a change of heart. And finally, reinvent a new result that you can hope for, a tangible service or product that you have envisioned.

Take note how this cycle isn't only a one-time process; you will continue this cycle as you continue living. The earlier chapters in this book have prepared you for exercising the three-step strategy. Here's a brief demonstration: if you want to adopt a healthy lifestyle for aging gracefully, you would *reflect* on your current eating habits; next, *imagine* yourself with more energy and increased stamina; and then you would *reinvent* your meals using the five golden rules of healthy eating (see Chapter 3).

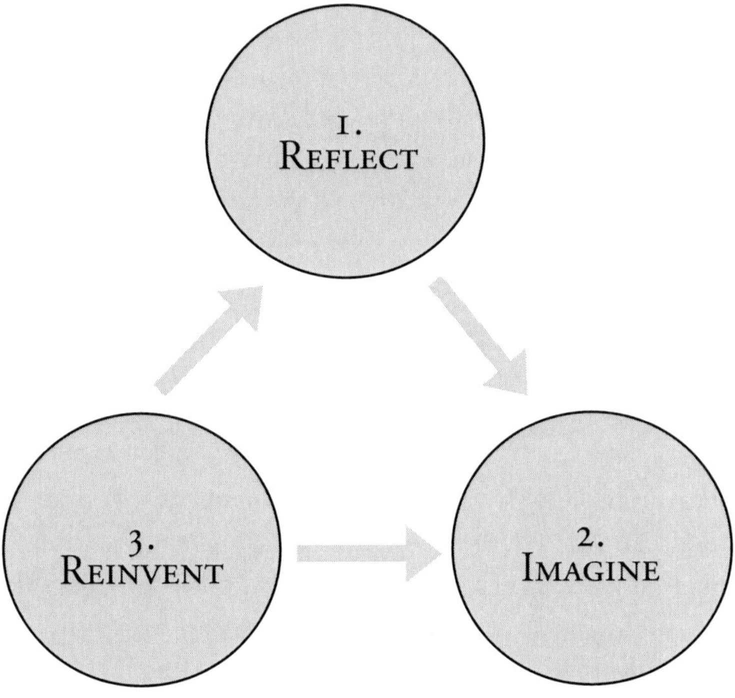

1. Reflect

Every day, we're swamped with breaking news, deadlines, emails, texts, social network feeds, and multiple demands from people and so on. Finding time to reflect is literally a luxury. This is a common feeling amongst many people—in a study of 50 participants over age 95, they agreed they would spend more time in reflection if they could do life over again. (See Chapter 1 for study synopsis.)

The Bible also teaches us to reflect. There are more than 200 references to "reflect" and "remember" in the scriptures: "reflect on what I am saying," "remember the poor," "remember the Lord your God," etc. Taking time to reflect on what we've read from the Bible or learned from a sermon is essential for spiritual growth and maturity.

The book of James imparts us to be "doers" of God's word rather than "hearers." We are expected to act on what we've learned from scriptures. James uses the analogy of someone forgetting his or her appearance after looking in a mirror. What's the point of looking in the mirror, then? If we read the Bible and do not practice the principles taught, what's the point of reading the Bible?

James' point is that when we look in the mirror, we see our reflection. Now look intently into God's word, the Bible: we see the perfect law of God that frees us from guilt, pain, and bondage, giving us hope for the present and future. As we keenly look at the perfect law (otherwise, the Bible), we see God's reflection—in particular, His love and righteousness. So upon your reflection, allow the imprint of Christ to shape the way you think and act. *"But whoever looks intently into the perfect law that gives freedom, and continues in it—not forgetting what they have heard, but doing it—they will be blessed in what they do"* (James 1:25).

To begin planning for your next steps, reflect on your assets and liabilities, including your passion, personality strengths, interests, life gifts, spiritual gifts, talents, skills, and potential concerns. Likewise, consider your future possibilities. The facts may not be readily available at your fingertips, so some research may be required. For example, if you're considering early retirement to start a second career, look into educational courses, investment options, and volunteer openings. Next, review the current status of your health, resources, priorities, and commitments. Answering the following questions may help you delve deeper into your reflection.

Review your current status, strengths, and opportunities

- What obligations are you still responsible for and for how long?
- What is your current health situation? Note any areas of concern.
- What is your current financial situation? Note any pitfalls to avoid.
- What are the possibilities and opportunities you will be interested in for the next five or 10 years?
- Which of your key assets will help support your opportunities and goals?

Review your potential weaknesses and pressures

- What does or will not work out when trying to live out your calling?
- What will threaten your ability to live out your calling in the near future?
- What can you do to minimize potential pitfalls?

Reflect on your calling

The next set of questions focuses on living out your calling. What were you made to do? To help you answer the following questions, review your life mission statement that you developed in Chapter 10. Or you can consider the dream board you might have already created (see Chapter 6).

- What is the focus of what you want to do? (Note: be very specific.

- What sorts of tasks will you be doing? What kinds of tasks will you not be doing? (Note: sometimes listing what we can or can't do helps us weed out activities that do not align with our calling.)
- How well are you currently living out your calling
- What else can you do to align yourself with your life calling?

2. Imagine

"Imagination is more important than knowledge," said Albert Einstein. Knowledge has a limit, whereas imagination does not. Seeing what you will become involves creative imagination. Following the strategies in Chapter 3, picture yourself on the cover of a Vitality-themed magazine. What do you see? What would you like to see?

Similar to the technique described in Chapter 9: Visualize to Achieve, here you will be envisioning your results before they happen. Imagine yourself aging gracefully, doing something that brings you utter joy. You do it not because you have to; you do it because you love it. It's your passion. It's your dream! Imagine how other people are benefiting from your wisdom, service, product, or innovation. As you imagine your desired state, describe it from spiritual, physical, emotional, and mental/intellectual perspectives.

Spiritual Example: I imagine myself trusting God, giving thanks to Him, and meditating on His loving grace.

Your Turn:

Physical Example: I imagine myself maintaining a work-life balance, being physically active, and making healthy lifestyle choices.

Your Turn:

Emotional Example: I imagine myself extending grace to others, practicing forgiveness, and managing stress.

Your Turn:

Mental/Intellectual Example: I imagine myself keeping busy with regular challenging mental activities. I am also intellectually engaged.

Your Turn:

Now refer to the first step of this exercise, which is your reflection. Is there a gap between your current state and your desired state? What needs to happen for your dream to come true? This leads to the third step: reinvent.

3. Reinvent

If you're unable to identify the steps for making your dream come true, it probably won't happen. Reinventing yourself takes effort, courage, and determination. Think hard, do your research, read books, take a course, and consult with experts. For instance, these are the steps I took a few years ago to prepare for this book: read articles and studied books on writing and publishing; attended a writing conference; wrote a book proposal, created a chapter-by-chapter synopsis; consulted with critique groups, authors, and mentors; worked with an editor, etc. See, it all started with a blank page. Faith, persistence, and patience kept me going and filling up one page at a time. During this reinvention process, I found it helpful to break down my goals into smaller deliverables, which were guided by milestones and target dates.

What are Deliverables, Milestones, and Target Dates?

A deliverable is a tangible output or result or a unit of work such as a report, a completed course, a sweater, a painting, or a wooden cabinet. A milestone is a significant event that indicates when an important landmark is reached. For example, your goal is to raise funds for cancer research by supporting the next charity gala event in December. You would set a target date of November 30th to complete a portfolio of five hand-knit sweaters and 10 scarves. However, this due date may seem like a long time away. To ensure you meet the final target, you would divide each task into milestone markers; this will state when each knit needs to be completed. In this example, you would organize your deliverables, milestones, and targets as:

Christmas Fundraising Project

Target Date:	*November 30*
Deliverable:	*5 hand-knit sweaters and 10 scarves*
Milestone 1:	*Complete 1st sweater by January 15*
Milestone 2:	*Complete 2nd sweater by February 10*

...

...

Final Milestone: *Complete the knitting portfolio by November 30*

My friend Ray is in the process of reinventing himself. He's transitioning his role from an international corporate trainer to a pastor. So he set aside three years to complete his seminary studies, which will help him reach his goal. He set these target dates and milestones to guide his planning process:

Ray's 2nd Career Dream

Date	***Milestone***	***Deliverable***
10-Dec-2010	*Complete application forms*	*Application Submission*
10-Feb-2011	*Complete references and recommendations*	*References Submission*
6-Sep-2011	*1st day of seminary school*	
10-May-2013	*Graduation – Master of Divinity*	*Degree in Divinity*
30-Jul-2013	*Complete a trip to the Orient*	
14-Sep-2013	*Launch ministry*	

To a lot of people, the fun part happens when the results are evident. For instance, completing a number of oil paintings is a tangible outcome for an artist, which is the result of many tasks leading up to it. Every finished painting puts that artist closer to her goal of presenting work in an art show. This may have been her major milestone that took five years to fulfill. As an artist, her life mission is to exemplify the beauty of this world by capturing nature on canvas. She will continue to enjoy her paintings as long as she lives.

Celebrating milestone achievements is necessary. We need encouragement and affirmation. This is also an excellent moment to reflect on your successes and lessons, as well as evaluate where you need to grow.

Just remember, plans may change. It's important to make allowances for unexpected events, and you may have to re-align your priorities. As discussed in Chapter 4, without a plan, it's like driving to an exotic place without a destination in mind.

Using your personal reflection (see Step 1), plan out your target dates, milestones (your significant event), and deliverables (your tangible output or result).

Your Turn

Target Date	Milestone	Deliverables

Reflect Back, Look Forward

In the business world, there is an evaluation phase in which project teams celebrate achievements, gather the lessons they learned, review challenges, and make future recommendations. The lessons they've learned not only include the things that went wrong. These also include successes that can be remembered for similar projects in the future. For parents, you may remember attending those teacher-parent interviews. The teacher would ask the student to proudly display his or her work and you would discuss your child's merits and improvement areas with the teacher.

I find this evaluation phase to be very helpful and applicable to our day-to-day living. We usually don't practice enough reflection. It's important for us to reflect, remember, and celebrate successes and learn from our past mistakes. Let's be proactive in applying this tool more often in our lives. Make it a habit to note each accomplishment, no matter how trivial it may seem.

We usually don't practice enough reflection. It's important for us to reflect, remember, and celebrate successes and learn from our past mistakes.

Noting Accomplishments

When our children were young, they brought home awards such as "student of the week," "craziest hair," "calligraphy master," "teacher's little helper" or "certificate of participation." But what happens when we get older? We can recognize our accomplishments in many other activities. These may include doing brisk walks three days in a row, eating tofu stir-fry instead of barbeque ribs on Mondays, patiently listening and attending to our elderly parents' needs, or saying something encouraging to the cashier at the supermarket checkout. If you like journaling, consider starting a section just for your accomplishments. You can keep the journal in a notebook or publish it on an online blog.

Counting Successes

We can learn from past successes. When we recall an event, we think of the tangible things that took place and the associated emotions. Here's an example you might be able to relate to: I remember the last time we held a family reunion at our house. The barbecue event was a smashing success. The spicy, juicy, tangy chicken wings turned out just right. The colorful grilled veggie kabobs and the mouth-watering watermelon salad were world-class. We also had salmon and sweet potatoes, and homemade ice cream for dessert. With the '70s music in the background, everyone shared stories well into the night. It was hard to say goodbye when the evening ended.

From this particular event, I learned what we could do for future endeavors. We definitely feel that having reunions in a home is a warm environment. We also agree that when we have similar events in the summer every year, we need to ensure that the chicken wings are marinated with the same Thai tangy sauce. So consider this thought: as we grow older, we have even more experience. Pay attention to what works well and make a mental note to repeat those similar deeds.

Noting Obstacles

We can also learn from our mistakes. Recalling what went wrong is not critical if we focus on "what happened" rather than "who did that." I remember an incident at work that caused me many sleepless nights. A staff member on my team filed a complaint against me to the human resources department. The complaint led to a series of review meetings and investigations into files and records.

Needless to say, the incident taught me valuable lessons that I was only privy to from reading textbooks or HR journals. I learned about company policies and processes that I never knew about before. So on the plus side, this made me appreciate the importance of sound HR practices.

The investigation was completed and the accusations against me were dismissed without any disciplinary actions. How would I do it differently next time around? I wrote down three pages of recommendations to myself in my journal: during one-on-one conversations, always clarify points and seek confirmation from the other party; do not assume your jokes are funny; and acknowledge other people's hard work.

Effective communication is the key to building harmony in relationships. There's so much to learn because whenever there are people, there are conflicts. My former staff member and I are friends today and we both came away from the incident as better people.

You may never have someone file a complaint against you. But you can always learn from formal or informal feedback. One example to consider is the role of a workshop facilitator. At the end of each workshop, he reviews comments from his students and event-organizing committee. He updates his workshop and promotional material based on these comments and creates action plans to improve on areas that he needs to upgrade. Take courage in learning from your errors. Act upon relevant feedback as part of reinventing yourself.

> First comes thought; then organization of that thought, into ideas and plans; then transformation of those plans into reality.
> –Napoleon Hill (1883–1970), American author

Ready, Set, Go

A few summers back, my family and I visited the Great Wall of China. I keenly remember tying the laces on hiking boots, packing some food and water, and away we went. We used many milestones as guideposts, which helped us identify how far we had come. Finally, with waving flags, we were thrilled to set foot on a 35-foot-tall watchtower, after striding along layers of bricks and muddy stones. When we looked down, we couldn't believe what we saw: pink, red, and violet blooming flowers and lush trees along the silvery brick walls—for miles and miles.

Every time we approached the end of a segment, a new one always began. We never reached the top of the mountain, but we celebrated our feats by counting the steps we climbed or remembering the fortresses we landed on.

> Reinventing yourself is like hiking up, down, and around the Great Wall of China.

Reinventing yourself is like hiking up, down, and around the Great Wall of China. You can't scale the Great Wall with a one-step leap to the top. But this doesn't mean you should stop reaching for your goal.

Growing and excelling to live out your calling is a process—you will not become an overnight sensation in achieving your target. Your passion is a strong motivator to cheer you through one step at a time. Be patient, sink into your soul, and watch how God leads you to higher ground.

Summary

Plan your work and work your plan. Regularly reflect on your status, strengths, weaknesses, opportunities, and threats; imagine the outcome you would like to see; then reinvent your reality with actions and tangible outputs. You will be able to focus your time on aspects that are most aligned with your calling. Launch your sail to leave a lasting legacy. Commit your plan to God. Execute your master plan faithfully.

But blessed is the one who trusts in the Lord, whose confidence is in him.
–Jeremiah 17:7

twelve

MAKE YOUR COMMITMENT

"Commit your way to the LORD, trust also in Him,
and He shall bring it to pass."
–Psalm 37:5, NKJV

"For the word of the LORD is right and true; he is faithful
in all he does."
–Psalm 33:4

SOMEONE ONCE DEFINED COMMITMENT AS BEING 100 PERCENT faithful to something or someone. Faith involves having confidence in what we hope for, believing in a person or a cause that is unseen or that hasn't happened yet. The Bible says, *"Commit to the LORD whatever you do, and he will establish your plans"* (Proverbs 16:3). We're instructed to put our trust in God and to make Him our first priority. He will bless our paths.

> As we reimagine our retirement, we need to be faithful in shaping and executing our plans to live out our calling.

As we reimagine our retirement, we need to be faithful in shaping and executing our plans to live out our calling. Taking a pledge to reinvent a new reality requires introspection, focus, and persistence. With that, we shall conquer the bumps along the way. Let's consider John's story.

Retirement Turnaround

John, a successful financial advisor and boomer, was vacationing in Cuba one summer with his wife. They rented a small boat to do a little snorkeling in the open water. On the boat was a strong, tanned, cheerful tour guide named Carlos, who was in his early 50s.

As they sat across from each other looking out into the serene sea, John was in awe of Carlos' peaceful demeanor. Usually surrounded by a hectic, fast-paced office environment, John wasn't used to being around someone so calm and easygoing. John just had to ask Carlos how he lived his life.

"Carlos, how many hours do you work each day?" John casually asked.

"I usually wake up around eight in the morning," Carlos answered. "I'm out at sea by 10 to take out a group of tourists like you. Then by two o'clock in the afternoon, I'm done for the day."

"How many children do you have?" John inquired.

With a proud grin, Carlos described his three grown children, adding how he enjoys spending his spare time playing with his grandchildren. He also spends his days going to the market with his wife, helping to prepare dinner, eating with his family and then mingling with his friends in the village square.

As a follower of Jesus Christ, John wondered if Carlos was a believer. John learned that Carlos was an atheist, which wasn't a surprise. John was well aware that only less than five percent of Cuba's population attends church. When the trip was over, John thanked Carlos for the boat ride—little did John know, his modest conversation with Carlos would impact him forever.

John came home to Canada. He immediately immersed himself in his business, attending to clients and managing account portfolios. Though full-time work kept John occupied, he was contemplating whether he should slow down his pace. After all, he was financially well off. His two grown sons were already independent professionals, living on their own. What was the point in working for money if he didn't need any more?

Suddenly, life took a sharp turn. John was diagnosed with stage 2 colorectal cancer. Fortunately, he was nurtured back to health a year after surgery. Then he was struck with a new outlook in life. One day, John will face his own destiny and it could come without any warning.

However, the thought of meeting God and reuniting with his Christian friends in heaven was reassuring; John did not have to fear death. Yet, he wondered about the many people who had no hope for paradise.

Swiftly, John reimagined his retirement years. All the while, images of Carlos and the Cuban sun came to mind. Carlos and his family needed to hear the good news of Jesus Christ. They, too, needed the hope of eternal life. John envisioned linking his faith to his retirement dream. But what was his retirement dream?

Lord, you are my God; I will exalt you and praise your name, for in perfect faithfulness you have done wonderful things, things planned long ago.
–Isaiah 25:1

After much praying and soul-searching, John realized that he needed to support international missionaries. He decided to take courses on mission and outreach, which opened his eyes to the needs of the world. The only real answer to suffering, poverty, injustice, and social problems lies in the salvation of the human soul.

John committed himself to study the Bible, to live out his faith, and to become a change agent of God. While he remained semi-retired, he volunteered for an organization dedicated to mission work in South America, including Cuba.

Three years later, John went back to Cuba to visit Carlos and his family. This time, they talked about faith. John shared God's love and care for him during his ordeal with cancer. Then John visited the church outside Havana, introducing Carlos to the pastor. He also bought Spanish Bibles for Carlos' family and encouraged them to join Bible study groups. Within a few months, Carlos and his family began attending church regularly.

Back home in Canada, John subscribed to quarterly magazines from the Cuban missionaries and continuously prayed for the churches there. A couple of years later, John learned that Carlos was privileged with the gift of eternal life. As he was flipping through a magazine, John found a glossy photo of Carlos under a section called "Inspiring Moments." In this picture, Carlos was getting baptized.

Today, John is a member of the board of the mission organization he volunteers for. Using his business skills, he is also the organization's financial consultant.

Remember how John wasn't sure about working for money much longer? Now, look what he's doing—he is finally living out his life calling, which is to serve global missionaries. This is a role John is good at and something he is passionate about.

Start Living Your Dream Today

Do not merely listen to the word, and so deceive yourselves. Do what it says.
–James 1:22

John is a fine example of a baby boomer living out his dream. And you can do this, too! You have a mission to accomplish: to live to your full potential and to leave a lasting legacy for the next generations. Whatever your calling is, start living it today.

This book has taken you through an amazing journey of yourself. You have an understanding of why God designed your identity and what you're capable of becoming. If you want to make a difference in someone's life, I encourage you to be an active participant rather than a passive spectator.

I trust that you are ready to commit your goals to the next stage of your earthly journey, especially to Him. Redefine your retirement by reimagining a God-inspired future.

My Prayer

I look forward to witnessing your wonders anew. I humbly invite you to join me in this prayer.

A Prayer of Commitment

The seasons of life wax and wane like a rolling wave.
Our lives are in your hands.
You protect.
You preserve.
You promote.
You prosper.

What can a person do to calm the mighty water?
What can a person do to rouse the crushing wind?
What can a person do to intrude the daring skyline?
What can a person do to beautify the transient rainbow?
What can a person give in exchange for an undeserved life?
What can a person yield in response to such a gift?

There is nothing more I want to do, except:
Offer myself to be your witness,
Attend to my family,
Act to free people from oppression,
Convey hope to the discouraged,
Serve the needy, the weak and the poor,
Bring glory to your name.

May people see you when seeing me!
May people hear you when hearing me!
May people know you when knowing me!
May people love you when loving me!

To your name be the glory!
Amen

endnotes

1. *Successful Aging* by John W. Rowe, M.D. and Robert L. Kahn, Ph.D. Published by Dell Publishing, a division of Random House Inc. New York, USA. 1998.

2. *An Essay on the Development of Christian Doctrine* – retrieved on Oct 26, 2012 http://www.newmanreader.org/works/development/index.html.

3. Exodus 7:7; Deuteronomy 34:7.

4. Genesis 17:15–22.

5. B.C. 1171 – 1060 according to p. 834 – *Young's Analytical Concordance to the Bible* by Robert Young, LL.D. revised by William B. Stevenson, B.D. and David Wimbish, B.S., Thomas Nelson Publishers, Nashville, USA.

6. 1 Samuel 7:15 to 8:1 (Samuel continued to Judge Israel all the days of his life and appointed his sons to rule Israel when he grew old); Samuel lived to anoint David as king to succeed Saul. 1 Samuel 13:1 (Saul was 30 years old when he became king and he ruled over Israel for 42 years.); 1King 2:11(David reigned for 40 years).

7. Sermon by Tony Campolo at Chatauqua Institution in Chatauqua, NY, on July 11, 2011 http://tonycampolo.org/sermons/2011/07/living-life-backwards/ retrieved on Oct 26, 2012.

8. *Working after age 65* http://www.policyalternatives.ca/sites/default/files/uploads/publications/National%20Office/2012/04/WorkingAfter65.pdf retrieved on Oct 26, 2012.

9. *Randstad Workmonitor Global Press Report Q4 2011* retrieved on Oct 26, 2012 p. 4, 5, 16 http://www.randstad.com/press-room/randstad-workmonitor/randstad-workmonitordecember2011.pdf.

10. Sun Life Financial news release on February 22, 2012. *Survey reveals only 30 per cent of Canadians expect to be fully retired at age 66* http://www.sunlife.ca/Canada/sunlifeCA/About+us/Media+centre/News+releases/2012/Survey+reveals+only+30+per+cent+of+Canadians+expect+to+be+fully+retired+at+age+66?vgnLocale=en CA retrieved in Oct 2012.

11. Chittister, Joan. *The Gift of Years: Growing Older Gracefully*, New York, NY: Bluebridge, 2008.

12. *Number of boomers working past retirement skyrockets.* Retrieved on Oct 27, 2012 http://business.financialpost.com/2011/09/29/number-of-boomers-working-past-retirement-skyrockets/.

13. For current Canadian Pension and Old Age Security rates, check the Service Canada website: http://www.servicecanada.gc.ca/eng/isp/pub/factsheets/rates.shtml.

14. Scott, Steven K. *The Richest Man Who Ever Lived: King Solomon's Secrets to Success, Wealth, and Happiness [Kindle Edition].* Random House Digital, Inc. 2006.

15. 1 Kings 3:5.

16. Matthew 25:14–30.

17. Niven, David. *100 Simple Secrets of the Best Half of Life: What scientists have learned and how you can use it* (California, USA: HarperSanFrancisco, 2005).

18. Cohen, Gene D., M.D., Ph.D. *The Mature Mind: The Power of the Aging Brain* (New York, USA: Basic Books, 2006), 57–87.

19. Bolles, Richard N. *The Three Boxes of Life and How to Get Out of Them* (California, USA: Ten Speed Press, 1981).

20. Laslett, Peter. *A Fresh Map of Life, 2nd Edition* (Suffolk, Great Britain: Macmillan Press Ltd. 1996) 177–202.

21. Georgia State University, Atlanta, USA. *Age differences in coping resources and satisfaction with life among middle-aged, young-old, and oldest-old adults.* The Journal of Genetic Psychology, 163(3), 360-367 Hamarat, E., Thompson, D., Aysan F., Steele D., Matheny, K., Simon, C. (2002).

22. Rowe, John W., Robert L. Kahn, *Successful Aging*. (New York, USA: Dell Publishing, a division of Random House Inc., 1998 Large Print Edition), 180–182.

23. Alzheimer Society website, Retrieved on Oct 27, 2012 http://www.alzheimertoronto.org/ad_Statistics.htm.

24. *2012 Alzheimer's Disease Facts and Figures,* p. 16. In 2012 statistics, Alzheimer's disease affects 1 in 8 people over the age of 65 and 45% of people over 85 and older has Alzheimer's. Retrieved on Oct 27, 2012 http://www.alz.org/downloads/facts_figures_2012.pdf.

25. Wood, Samuel E. et al. *The World of Psychology. Updated 3rd Canadian Edition* (Ontario, Canada: Pearson Allynand Bacon 2004), 214.

26. Duffy, Karen G., Eastwood Atwater. *Psychology for Living. 8th Edition.* (New Jersey, USA: Upper Saddle River, 2004), 78–79.

27. Duffy, Karen G., Eastwood Atwater. *Psychology for Living. 8th Edition.* (New Jersey, USA: Upper Saddle River, 2004), 78–79.

28. Wood, Samuel E. et al. *The World of Psychology. Updated 3rd Canadian Edition.* (Ontario, Canada: Pearson Allynand Bacon 2004), 217.

29. Goleman, Daniel. *Emotional Intelligence. The 10th Anniversary Edition.* (New York, USA Bantam Books 2006), 227–228.

30. Rubin, Lillian B., *60 On Up: The Truth About Aging in America.* (Massachusetts, USA: Beacon Press Books, 2007), 8.

31. Weil Andrew. Healthy Aging: *A lifelong guide to your physical and spiritual well-being.* (New York, USA: Knopf, Borzoi Books, 2005), 5–6.

32. McMillen, S.I. and Stern, David E. *None of These Diseases.* (Michigan, USA: Fleming H. Revell, 1963, 1984, 2000), 167–177.

33. Duff, Clarence. *Unlock the Mystery of Depression.* (Ontario, Canada: Essence Publishing, 2003), 79–81.

34. Public Health Agency Website, retrieved on Oct 27, 2012 http://www.phac-aspc.gc.ca/hp-ps/hl-mvs/pa-ap/index-eng.php.

35. Rivlin, Richard S. *Keeping the young-elderly healthy: is it too late to improve our health through nutrition?* American *Journal of Clinical Nutrition,* November 2007 vol. 86 no. 5 1572S-1576S.

36. Colbert, Don. *Deadly Emotions: Understand the Mind-Body-Spirit connection that can heal or destroy you* (Tennessee, USA: Thomas Nelson Inc. 2003).

37. Nouwen, Henri J.M. *Making All Things New: An Invitation to the Spiritual Life.* (New York, USA: Harper & Row Publishers, Inc. 1981), 28.

38. McMillen, S.I. and Stern, David E. *None of These Diseases.* (Michigan, USA: Fleming H. Revell, 1963, 1984, 2000), 199.

39. Study: *Positive images of old age conducive to long life*. Retrieved on Oct 27, 2012 http://www.yale.edu/opa/arc-ybc/v31.n1/story10.html.

40. Dweck, Carol S. Mindset*: The New Psychology of Success – How we can learn to fulfill our potential* (New York, USA: Ballantine Books Reprint Edition 2008), 6–8.

41. Statistics Canada report. *Delayed Retirement: a New Trend,* published on Oct 26, 2011. P. 12. Retrieved on Oct 27, 2012 http://www.statcan.gc.ca/pub/75-001-x/20one hundred and ten-4/article/11578-eng.pdf.

42. Crowe, Andy. *Alpha Project Managers: What the Top 2% Know That Everyone Else Does Not* (Georgia, USA: Velociteach, 2006).

43. World Health Organization website. *50 Facts: Global health situation and trends 1955-2025* Retrieved on Oct 27, 2012. http://www.who.int/whr/1998/media_centre/50facts/en/.

44. Kise, Jane A.G., David Stark, Sandra Krebs Hirsh. *Discover Who You Are* (Minnesota, USA: Bethany House Publishers, 1996, 2005), 38–39.

45. Online resource on RIASEC Inventory tool. Retrieved on Oct 28, 2012. http://www.career-lifeskills.com/pdf/jst-576530-guide.pdf.

46. Kise, Jane A.G., David Stark, Sandra Krebs Hirsh. *Discover Who You Are* (Minnesota, USA: Bethany House Publishers, 1996, 2005), 48–71.

47. Wagner, Peter C. *Discover Your Spiritual Gifts* (California, USA: Regal Books, 2002, 2005), 107.

48. Wagner, Peter C. *Discover Your Spiritual Gifts* (California, USA: Regal Books, 2002, 2005), 108–115.

49. Littauer, Marita, Florence Littauer. *Wired That Way* (California, USA: Regal Books, 2006), 16–22.

50. Littauer, Florence. *Personality Plus: How to Understand Others by Understanding Yourself* (Michigan, USA: Revell, 1983, 1992), 142–148.

51. Littauer, Marita, Florence Littauer. *Wired That Way* (California, USA: Regal Books, 2006), 96–105.

52. LaHaye, Tim. *Spirit-Controlled Temperament* (Illinois, USA: Tyndale House Publishers, Inc. 1966, 1992, 1994), 109–126.

53. Littauer, Florence. *Personality Plus: How to Understand Others by Understanding Yourself* (Michigan, USA: Revell, 1983, 1992), 191.

54. Mui, Anita. Retrieved on Oct 27, 2012. http://www.encyclopedia.com/doc/1G2-3430100046.html.

55. Littauer, Florence. *Your Personality Tree* (Tennessee, USA: Thomas Nelson, 1986), 215.

56. Article: Apr 21, 2012, *George Beverly Shea singing God's praise at 103.* Retrieved on Oct 28, 2012. http://www.wnd.com/2012/04/george-beverly-shea-singing-gods-praise-at-103/.

57. *Operation Multiplication.* Retrieved on Oct 28, 2012. http://www.ieaom.org/whatisom.html.

58. Jones, Laura Beth. *The Path: Creating Your Mission Statement for Work and for Life* (New York, USA: Hyperion, 1996), 3–25.

acknowledgements

I KISSED MY MOM GOODBYE AT THE AIRPORT AS SHE LEFT FOR A warmer place, dodging the Canadian winter. The night before, Mom handed me a red packet with a $50 bill and wished me success on my upcoming book launch. Yeah, Mom is my first customer preordering my book. She does not know English! I thank my parents, my biggest fans in everything I do.

My husband Philip and daughter Amanda diligently keep the house and meals in order as I immerse myself in researching, writing, and editing. Ginny, Sam, Michelle, and Isaac are my faithful supporters, always responding to my queries. Thanks for your love and support.

Can I claim that this book is a result of my hard work? Yes and no. Without the wisdom, guidance, and encouragement from a few key people, I would have just completed some serious writing but not a book.

I'll start by acknowledging Nikki Yeh, my editorial confidant, sounding board, and young professional friend. Nikki offered many insightful suggestions and meticulous editorial comments that solidified the book concept as compiled in the original book proposal and manuscript draft. Two other mentors, Ray Wiseman and Mary Lou Cornish, guided me with tips and techniques, wise counsel, and manuscript critiques. They encouraged me to follow my passion and keep writing.

Last but not least, without the support from the professional and friendly staff of Word Alive Press, this book would not have succeeded in final editing, cover design, book layout design, production and distribution. Thanks to all of you, Tiffany, Tom, Greg, Nikki, Kylee, Janelle, and Cindy.

about the author

PROFESSIONALLY, JOYCE IS A PROJECT MANAGER, CONSULTANT, motivational speaker, teacher, and an author. Personally, she has been married to Philip for 30 years and they have four grown children. The secret to her marriage and parenting is one and the same: faithful teamwork.

Joyce models lifelong learning. In 1980, she graduated from California State University, Fresno, with a bachelor of science in business administration. Joyce entered the workforce as a computer programmer and developed expertise in Information Technology over the years. She became a wife and a mother of four lovely children—all without giving up a challenging career. While raising her family with husband Philip, Joyce began part-time graduate school at the age of 40. In 2004, she attained a master's degree in Christian counseling from Canada Christian College. She then completed a doctorate in philosophy in international missions and counseling through distance and modular education from California State Christian University in 2006. Joyce continues her learning journey studying Traditional Chinese Medicine part-time.

Joyce is passionate in motivating others to live out their full potential. Currently, Joyce works as a project management consultant and she facilitates personal development workshops under her business, Fullness of Life Consulting. Joyce and Philip live in Brampton, Ontario, Canada.

Joyce enjoys speaking for churches and organizations. To view a list of her favorite speaking topics or to book Joyce for events, workshops or retreats, visit her website: www.fullnessoflife.com.

Call-out from Joyce

I hope you enjoy *Reimagine Your Retirement.* I'd love to hear your thoughts, your journey, and your own story as you reimagine your retirement. You and I are committed to contribute and make a difference in someone's life. It takes all of us to make this world a better place. Let's continue to encourage each other by keeping in touch. Visit my blog: www.fullnessoflife.com/blog to:

1) Leave me a comment about this book, your experience, or your questions, etc.
2) Sign up for my monthly newsletter
3) Read and comment on my blog
4) Order additional copies of the book for your friends or your church group as study material